Phenomenal Men of FAITH

10 INSPIRING STORIES WRITTEN BY 10 PHENOMENAL MEN

Copyright © 2024 BFF Publishing House, LLC
Printed in the United States of America
Email address: bff@bffpublishinghouse.com
Website: www.bffpublishinghouse.com

Scriptures are taken from the Holy Bible, New International Version, NIV, Copyright 1973, 1978, 2011 by Biblica, Inc. All rights reserved worldwide. The "NIV" and "New International Version" are trademarks registered in the United States Patent and Trademark Office by Biblica, Inc.

Scripture marked NKJV are from the New Kings James Version, Copyright 1982 by Thomas Nelson. All rights reserved. Scriptures marked NLT are from the Holy Bible, New Living Translation. 1996, 2004, 2007, 2013, 2015 by Tyndale House Foundation. Tyndale House Publishers, Carol Stream, Illinois 60188. All rights reserved.

Disclaimer: This book is the author's personal, non-fictional story. Every account in the book is true, and the events are portrayed to the best of the author's memory. While all the stories in this book are true, names and identifying details were eliminated to protect the privacy of the people involved. The author does not assume and hereby disclaims any liability to any party for any loss, damage, emotional distress, or disruption as a result of the book content.

Any internet addresses, books, products, blogs are offered as a resource and not intended in any way to imply an endorsement by BFF Publishing House.

Printed in the United States of America. All rights reserved under international Copyright Law. Contents and/or cover may not be reproduced in whole or in any form without the express written consent of the Publisher, expect by a reviewer, who may quote brief passages in connection with a review for a magazine or newspaper.

BFF Publishing House is a Limited Liability Corporation dedicated wholly to the appreciation and publication of books for children and adults for the advancement of diversification in literature.

For more information on publishing contact:
Antionette Mutcherson at
bff@bffpublishinghouse.com
Website: bffpublishinghouse.com
Published in the United States by
BFF Publishing House
Atlanta, Georgia First Edition, 2024

ISBN: 979-8-9890667-3-5

To My Father, Anthony (Tony) Ricardo Mutcherson

January 7, 1960 – October 16, 2021

It could not have been easy for you to experience life as a Black man with all of the travails you encountered. But you ascended . . . phenomenally. I honor you with this book filled with stories similar to yours.

I love you and miss you beyond this world, and I pray and endeavor that you feel me in yours.

Love,

Antionette (Toni) Mutcherson

Contents

Chapter 1: Spiritual Conviction
Carlos Scott, MBA 1

Chapter 2: Unpacking Boxes
Stephen Churn 25

Chapter 3: Family Matters
Sir Pegues, Ph.D., LPC, CPCS 51

Chapter 4: Don't Let a Good Life Stop You from Living a Great Life
Charles Prater 83

Chapter 5: Standing Tall by the Grace of God
Eric Jefferies 103

Chapter 6: Humbled by Experience
Cornelius Williams 131

Chapter 7: Spiritual Titan
Jared Fields, MPA 149

Chapter 8: Unveiling Faith: Lessons from the Journey
Corey Hackett 169

Chapter 9: Proof Is in the Progress
Rudy A. Simpson Jr. 195

Chapter 10: Faith Without Ceasing
Pastor Jerome Adkins 213

The Phenomenal Book Series 229

The BFF Publishing House Team 231

Chapter 1

SPIRITUAL CONVICTION

The parking lot of the Applebee's had never felt ominous in any of my countless prior visits there, but at that very moment, it was the most dreadful place on earth. Sure—inside, it was just a typical Friday night at your local chain establishment. There were tables filled with families enjoying platters of baby back ribs, couples splitting sizzling butter pecan blondies, and a bar full of individuals downing spirits to lift theirs up. But outside—in my car, more specifically—there was a ball of anxiety manifesting in the form of a butterfly in my stomach that felt as if it was the size of a pterodactyl and cold beads of sweat running down my spine from perspiration despite having the A/C on max.

I was a well-versed wordsmith amongst my peers, yet there I sat, speechless. I had exhausted all the courage I managed to muster up for the dialogue, merely inviting her to meet me for what was sure to be a dinner like none other. My eyes were locked on all entrances, as if glaring at them would suspend time briefly, all the while anticipating the moment I would see the vehicle carrying the one person who had more faith in me than anyone else—my mom.

Once inside, we shared our usual embrace and requested a booth per our tradition. I attempted to make light-hearted small talk, which I'm sure she saw right through, being that she was quite familiar with the mindless chatter I used to prime her for things I wanted throughout my entire life, typically to request a purchase be made or permission be given. Yet, tonight, there was no word salad I could serve her that would help her digest what I was about to say. Finally, after consuming what, unbeknownst to me, would be my last orange chicken bowl down to the last morsel in an effort to stall, I assumed a solemn tone and began to tell my mom the three words no parent ever wants to hear their child say: "I'm in trouble . . ."

That Friday, I had to tell my mom, who served as the sole reference and reason for my hiring, that I had been fired for the first time in my life by the same employer whom she had built a thirty-plus-year career with. Not only was I fired, but I had been assured that criminal charges and a warrant for my arrest would be issued at any moment. After detailing the depth of my stupidity and unconscionable actions to my mom as she sat tearfully marinating over the reality of what I shared, I began to become overcome with a grief like I never felt before.

It felt as if the entire restaurant's fixture joined her in mourning as the random trinkets and local high school paraphernalia all melted into blurs replaced by blotches of darkness surrounding my mother. I felt as if I had witnessed my mom attend my own funeral and burial within a blink of an eye. I had failed her and feared she had lost all faith in me.

Her only child, her pride and joy, the pastor's kid, the Student of the Year, the Presidential and Bright Futures full scholarship recipient . . . under investigation and facing incarceration. Needless to say, there was no splitting of any sizzling butter pecan blondie that evening. Instead, we both shared a dish of disbelief as we both wrestled with the fact that no matter what the outcome was, my life would never be the same.

After that evening, my relationship with my mother was never the same. Most would assume that to be negative, but I believe in that moment of honesty, I evolved into a version of myself that had nothing else to hide, thus allowing me to be myself with my mother like never before. I would soon come to find that as my legal woes unfolded, many of my friends and family would lose faith in me and presumed I would become another statistic. The support that she pledged as we departed that evening was soon thereafter tried and tested but to this day has never wavered. Unfortunately, I cannot say the same for my faith.

The weeks and months that followed were all littered with the certainty of imprisonment. Despite my efforts to try to continue living life as though my world wasn't crumbling around me, I was beginning to find myself questioning everything, including my faith. Several of my codefendants were arrested, and as word began to spread, I knew it was only a matter of time before my day would soon come. Nonetheless, I went on about my life and tried to savor and enjoy what I thought could be the last days. The last days of my innocence. The last days of my freedom.

. . . Until, one day, they came for me. It was the day before our final exams began, and I was just nonchalantly going about my regular routine as a college student: actively trying to engage in the subject matter taught by a professor whom, as an aside, I desired to make a lasting mark with for future fraternal ambitions. Unbeknownst to me, it was that day that the warrant for my arrest and orders for my detainment had been issued. This day was supposed to be a day I was prepared for, but I was everything but that. I had acquired legal counsel and was living under the auspices that my attorney would be notified prior to the execution of the warrant so we could arrange for me to turn myself in. Unfortunately, that was not the case.

Instead, the university's campus police rushed into the lecture hall, abruptly interrupting our professor and his lesson. As the officer whispered to our professor, it slowly dawned on me that this was it, and by the time my professor turned his attention in my direction, I had already begun gathering my things, awaiting further direction. I was then asked to accompany the officer, and once outside the classroom, I knew I wasn't going to be returning nor would the opportunity to build a rapport with a future fraternity brother serving as the advisor to a chapter I sought admission to join. I felt in that moment, he lost what little faith he had in me, if any, to join his esteemed organization.

The officer asked me to walk with him to his car, and for some reason, he attempted to preserve what little dignity I had remaining by not placing me under arrest until we got to his patrol car. As we walked through the grounds of the renowned business school and made our way down the hallways where I had spent the last three years preparing for my future in the business arena, I couldn't shake the feeling that I had officially messed my business up.

Once we finally arrived at the officer's patrol car, the officer then placed my wrists into a makeshift set of handcuffs made out of a zip tie and sat me in the back of the vehicle. The ride through campus was surreal, although brief, but I had enough time to come to the realization that I was not going to make it through the uncertainty of tomorrow without reaffirming my faith on that day. After waiting inside the campus precinct for a few minutes, the officer who'd escorted me turned to me with a somber look on his face and said, "I don't know what you did, but you got yourself in some serious trouble, son . . ."

Up until that moment, nobody had informed me of what I was being charged with or read me my Miranda Rights. Nonetheless, I knew them by heart from every pop culture reference related to police, but I knew the right to remain silent would not be waived regardless. When the officer told me how many charges I was facing, I was in utter disbelief. Some of my codefendants had already been charged, and I was expecting to receive similar if not slightly more, but I lacked the mental capacity to process what I was told at that moment.

For my first offense, I was charged with one hundred and three felonies. Let me repeat: 1-0-3 felony counts. The numbness that I was overcome by when I first heard that number was unforgettable. All the efforts to prepare myself mentally, physically, and spiritually fell short, and I was left in a state of the highest level of distress life could offer.

I was expecting multiple counts due to the manner in which my codefendants had been charged. Because of the role I played, I was going to take the brunt of the prosecution's attention, and they had no intention of taking it easy on me. The charges resulted in a bail bond totaling $130,000, which meant I would require just over $13,000 just to be released on bond.

As I sat in the holding cell, waiting to be placed in general population, the realization set in that I was not going to walk away from this ordeal unscathed. My bail amount was not something I nor my mother had readily available, so I wasn't expecting to see the outside of Leon County Jail anytime soon. After a sleepless night filled with prayers of repentance inside my cell, I heard a correctional officer call my name at around 6 a.m. to inform me that someone had posted bond for me.

I was shocked that $13,000 was able to be pooled together to get me out of a situation I'd put myself into. As I began to get processed for release, the officers at the jail began making comments about how I made bond so fast with such a high amount of bail set. "I would've bet my last dollar you weren't going anywhere unless they lowered your bond . . ." one lady officer said with a grin. Another officer seemed more concerned with my origins. "You must be related to someone famous or something . . . Who yo' people?" said the overweight officer with a silent "boy" at the end. (I didn't hear him say it, but I felt it, and it was very much implied.)

I was still holding firm to my right to remain silent and said nothing, although in actuality, I was racking my brain trying to guess what combination of funds was collected in order for me to not even spend twenty-four hours in jail after being charged in such a fashion. They said they hadn't ever seen anyone post bail that quickly with an amount that large, which, in hindsight, only makes me appreciate the lengths my mother, friends, and family went through to get me released.

I made my way through the exit of the facility and was greeted by my mother and a now former girlfriend. After reuniting and sharing a short moment of relief, we made our way to the bondsman, where I was then given the terms of my release and signed a ton of papers—one for every count I had been charged with, I believe. Then, I was informed my bail had been paid for hours ago, but my paperwork was so massive that it took them an exorbitant amount of time to process.

I was overcome with a sense of gratitude for all those who scraped, scrounged, and sacrificed to ensure I was released and didn't remain imprisoned while awaiting my case to move forward. I will forever remain indebted to those who contributed in that moment and beyond for their unwavering support of me even while I was at my lowest point in my life. Without any hesitation or judgment, they adhered to the call and sent/lent whatever was needed for my immediate release.

After a quick shower and without any rest, I returned to my regular scheduled programming and took an exam, although nothing was ever regular about my time in school from then on. While others were stressing over the grueling demands of finals week, I was existing in a state of an eternal anxiety attack for fear of losing freedom. By now, all those who cared to know had found out, either from the local newscast that plastered my face for all residents to see as they detailed the allegations levied against me or via word of mouth.

My home city, albeit the capital of the state, is truly more of a town than a city, and you can make big news in a small town. Nonetheless, I continued to live the life I was living and attempted to savor every second of my freedom until it was taken away from me. Wherever I was—school, work (which, at the time, was in the stockroom at a Victoria's Secret, but that's a story for another book)—I went about my days constantly masking my anxiety and depression to others and myself.

Masking my inner turmoil became as second nature as breathing. It was one of several coping mechanisms I employed to refrain from going AWOL and insane. But above all else, I had to persevere for those who'd just sacrificed for me to be back on the other side of the fence. For those who had unwavering faith in me and didn't believe that any sentence given to me by a judge or jury would be the last in my life's story.

As with most criminal charges, I was offered an initial plea deal from the prosecuting attorney. My knowledge of plea deals had instilled in me that the first offer was always the best offer, so with that in mind, I walked into my attorney's office with a bit of optimism despite the egregious amount of charges I was facing. It was my first offense, non-violent, non-sexual; just a white-collar crime committed while still of the age to be deemed a youthful offender.

On paper, I was an upstanding citizen, a native of the city, and enrolled at the local HBCU, excelling academically while maintaining a full-time job. In my mind, the initial plea offer would be something like a few years of supervised probation and some community service hours. The district attorney had something else in mind, though. My attorney informed me that the plea deal we received was for ten years of confinement and five years of supervised probation—fifteen years total.

Whatever I thought I knew about faith before that moment paled in comparison to the faith I clung to when I rejected the plea deal that day, knowing that a trial either by judge or jury could result in a sentence that surpassed the plea I was offered. In fact, the district attorney didn't mince words when he informed my attorney that if I went to trial, he was going to seek the maximum penalty. Coming to terms with the DA's utter disdain for me was a sobering moment that I wasn't prepared for. It was the first time that I felt as though my academic achievements and community engagement were held against me. In the eyes of the DA, my profile didn't align with the crimes I was charged with, and that just made it even more egregious to them.

I had dabbled in unsavory and illegal activities as a minor but was fortunate to never have any run-ins with the law. In fact, the offenses I was charged with paled in comparison to my prior transgressions, which I will refrain from elaborating on, and were deemed "white-collar" crimes. Nonetheless, the charges were not going to be reduced or dropped as long as the DA had a say in it, and at this point, most of my codefendants had taken pleas and agreed to testify against me as state witnesses if I were to go to trial, including a now ex-girlfriend. The DA was dead set on throwing the book at me, and as more of my codefendants continued to take plea deals, the potential for me to go to trial and win was very bleak.

The compounded stress of the case along with my attempts to maintain my day-to-day routine of school and work and my pursuit to pledge a fraternity left me in a constant state of anxiety. Every second that my attention wasn't required for the task before me was spent pondering my fate, questioning my purpose, doubting my self-worth, and marinating in shame. For months, I lived on the edge of my seat, not knowing if my next hearing would be my last. With every passing day, I made a concerted effort to live my life to the fullest for fear that it would be my last before my life changed forever.

Despite all my efforts to seize life by the horns, there were valleys I found myself dwelling in, overcome with a sense of hopelessness. My faith was put to the test like none before as I wrestled with remorse and shame while simultaneously asking for forgiveness and mercy from the Most High.

Thoughts of fleeing prosecution and running from my legal woes were amongst the many issues stirring internal strife within me. Even my life's worth and if my loved ones would be better off without me in this realm crossed my mind from time to time in my weakest moments. My faith was on a roller coaster, and for every peak, it seemed as if there were five times as many valleys.

Failure was not something I came to know as a youth and into my early adulthood. My faith was equally matched by my work to ensure my success in the classroom and in any other arena I entered. Even in the midst of a trial, due to my prior achievements and ambitions, I managed to be selected to join an illustrious Black Greek organization and pledge for months with charges looming, not knowing if I would even be free at the conclusion of the process. I struggled to accept that this was not a situation I would walk away from unblemished or without consequence. I felt that I had failed my faith and all the efforts I had made up until these charges were for naught.

As the date of my court appearance loomed, my attorney made a discovery that shifted the case drastically. They informed me that the actual charges I was given were not properly filed. The law I was accused of breaking stated that a certain threshold had to be reached per count. The State attempted to overlook that portion of the statute and instead charged me and my codefendants with multiple counts.

The total amount of funds that we were charged for taking did not warrant the amount of charges filed. Thus, only **one** charge should have been filed. My attorney informed me the day before my plea was to be entered, and when I heard the charges could be dropped from one hundred and three to one, I was astonished and overwhelmed. Something as simple as reading the statute in totality to comprehend the charges managed to evade all of the attorneys that my codefendants used, and my attorney was hours away from making the same costly oversight, too.

The morning of my final plea hearing was solemn. With each step I took, I questioned if it was my last as a free man or a convicted felon. As I entered the courtroom, accompanied by my mother and then-girlfriend, I was in a trance and numb. The technicality my attorney uncovered was my fail-safe, yet my anxiety was at an all-time high. I had placed all my faith in this defense and prayed more in the past eight months than my entire life, which is saying a lot, considering I had spent twenty-three years as the son of a Pentecostal pastor and missionary. The day was finally here. No more discovery hearings; no more plea negotiations. It was time to take a plea or set a trial date.

While my attorney and the DA discussed the findings and negotiated a better plea, I waited with a stomach full of butterflies with beads of sweat running down my back from anxiety. I had spent the last few months attempting to reaffirm my faith and praying for a favorable outcome. This was the moment that would possibly shift the weight of my case to a more palatable resolution for me.

I had put all my faith in my attorney, who had become my fraternity brother during the prior months, and even spent a considerable amount of time praying for the state attorney on the other side of the table, despite their prior efforts to have me confined for a period that would make an "example" out of any future "Robin Hood," as the investigators and DA had dubbed me. To them, I was the modern "spook who sat by the door," and my perversion of the system to aid and reparate others was egregious and despicable in their eyes. Nonetheless, I still leaned on my faith.

The door to the conference room opened, and the DA was first to depart. He shuffled by me without even acknowledging my existence and appeared to have been a few shades redder than I recall seeing him previously. I stood up, anticipating my attorney emerging from the room with a stride of victory, but instead saw a look of dissatisfaction and defeat as he slowly approached me. Before he could utter a single word, I knew that their conversation did not end favorably.

After a few moments of priming me, my attorney began to recap the conversation he had with the prosecutor. Despite agreeing that the charges were incorrect and the statues supported the reduction of counts, the DA was refusing to offer a reasonable plea. The fact that all of my codefendants had taken pleas and been charged with numerous counts prior to me being charged would have made several parties look quite foolish, including every attorney that took payment to defend my codefendants for failing to merely READ the actual law we were accused of breaking.

For me to be viewed as the central hub for the operation or, as it was explained to me in doodle art fashion, the center of a wheel full of spokes, to then get the lease amount of charges and have the right to potentially less severe sentencing boiled the state attorney's blood. It was written all over his face after the conclusion of their conference. He was so enraged at the idea of me not having to take on all that he had charged me with that he retorted with an ultimatum that would change my life forever.

The prosecutor was willing to drop two charges that, per the statute, were a prerequisite to the overarching charge. These couldn't be charged separately, thus reducing my charges to one hundred and one felonies with a plea deal of two years in confinement with the option to participate in the State's bed rest program upon completing the first ninety days of my bid. However, they refused to reduce the charges and give me one count, as prescribed by law, without rescinding my plea deal. He wanted to take me to trial, and he sought the maximum penalty of fifteen years imprisonment for me.

The state attorney had tipped his hand and shared their plans to have a parade of indirect victims take the stand one after another to convince the jury of the real-life impact my actions had on those throughout the state. He planned to top it off with the testimony of their star witness, my ex-girlfriend. His intentions were to clearly dissuade me from considering a trial. It was now time to decide: Either risk fifteen years of my life by going to trial, or take over one hundred felony charges and have the opportunity to work and rejoin society for twelve hours, six days a week for the next two years.

I was distraught and in disbelief. I had to choose my fate before the start of the hearing that day. There was no time to sleep on it or reschedule. I had to make the hardest choice of my life and choose between my record or my time.

I entered the courtroom and found a seat in the gallery among a cast of random people as my attorney joined a pew of defense attorneys. "All rise . . ." said the bailiff as the judge appeared from his chamber in a shirt and tie, still clothing himself in the customary black robe, somewhat humanizing him from the power and authority typically projected. After getting himself situated, he began to call out cases until, finally, he uttered, "The State versus Carlos Scott." I stood up and entered the courtroom floor and was joined by my attorney as the judge began to read each count I was being charged with out loud. Somewhere after the thirtieth count or so, I tuned out the drab voice of the judge, and my ears caught the gasps and reactions of those in the gallery.

"Daaaayum!" I heard whispered from behind me amongst a scattering of other comments while I gazed across the room at the courtroom clerks and personnel, who were also unable to contain their reactions. By the time the judge read all the counts, I felt as if I had unanimously become everyone's number one topic for discussion over dinner.

The state attorney offered his reduction of two charges, and it just made the entire ordeal seem that much more comical, as if he was doing me a favor by leaving me with only one hundred and one felonies. Then, the judge went on to read the State's plea offer, which, by that time, I had committed every word of to memory after anguishing over the decision I had come to.

My attorney looked at me one final time to confirm if I was ready to proceed with my response. Although my attorney knew I had come to terms with my decision, he maintained a battle-ready demeanor, instilling confidence that if I elected to turn course, he would happily hit play and serenade the courthouse with "Trial Time" by The Last Mr. Bigg. Alas, I casted aside the last bit of reservation I held and nodded my head for us to proceed as planned.

As the judge began to direct his line of questioning toward me and I responded accordingly, I thought of all the individuals who had poured into my life and all the faith they had for me. I thought of all the hours I had spent faithfully committed to academic excellence with the full understanding that it had a direct link to my future financial state; the years that I had lived as 'a "pastor's kid" with a legion of spiritual leaders who had spoken blessings over my life and prayed for God to order my steps; all the hands full of anointed oil that had been laid on me for as far back as I remembered—all of the efforts my village made to keep me from becoming the very statistic I had become. After the judge finished reviewing the terms of my pleas and a brief debate ensued over whether my charges were to be fully adjudicated or if the judge would withhold adjudication, the judge proceeded with declaring my charges all fully adjudicated, meaning no matter how much time I served, I could never have my charges concealed or expunged.

This one final blow from the State was intended to eradicate any hopes of me gaining meaningful employment and meant that I would spend the rest of my life being defined by my record, a lifelong stain my name would bear that would impede my ability to achieve any semblance of normalcy without enduring much strife. It paved the path for future employers to disregard my applications for employment and allowed property managers and housing institutions to deny me housing or increase move-in fees and security deposits without merit.

It would strip me of the opportunity to vote and participate in local and national elections as well as leave me legally defenseless from protecting myself and loved ones with a firearm. It was meant to be the knife to the throat of my future in juxtaposition to my education and early successful business endeavors. For those who couldn't get past my past, family and friends alike, I was either discarded and excommunicated for the shame I had brought upon myself and, in their view, them by association.

"You better be a damn good businessman . . ." my attorney said once we exited the courtroom that day. He had managed to have the judge grant our request to begin my sentence a few months from that hearing date, so I was fortunate to have the ability to get my affairs in order. But in turn, I had to pay $92,000 in restitution and court costs before the first day of my sentence.

This was obviously a financial burden on me and anyone in the vicinity who cared for me as I fundraised to account for more damages than I was truly responsible for. After meeting the court's terms and conditions and putting myself and loved ones in financial ruin, I spent the weeks that followed living like every day was my last. I continued to work multiple jobs and seek additional streams of income through my business ventures, but I could have quite possibly redefined "Eat, drink, and be merry" that summer, and by the time the day came for me to turn myself in, I had already made peace with my fate.

Although the next two years of my life would be spent incarcerated, I found solace in knowing that I was going to be held at a facility less than thirty minutes away from home and that I would be eligible for work release, provided I stayed clear of any issues during my first ninety days. Despite almost all of my prayers seemingly going unanswered during my trial, I found myself closer to God and reaffirmed my faith throughout all of my literal trials and tribulations. Even in the midst of my darkest hours, blessings still were bestowed upon me.

I gained a host of fraternity brothers who uplifted me while my trial and pledge process coincided. I gained a lifelong friend who I met while incarcerated; had it not been for his companionship, my time served would have been altered drastically. I also gained the space to commit mentally to several things and rekindled my passion for reading and writing. I began reading as many as three books a week. I took the cliché, "Do the time, don't let the time do you," to heart and vowed to make the most of my time and return from my sentence renewed, dubbing my entire bid as a setback for a setup to come back.

After the first ninety days of my sentence were completed, I was able to join the work release program and was allowed to work outside of the facility six days a week. For twelve hours, from 6 a.m. to 6 p.m. Monday through Saturday, I was able to rejoin society, and just as I made the most of my time inside, I made sure to do the same on the outside. The fall semester had already begun, but I made provision to return to the classroom in the spring, which put me in a rather precarious position for the remainder of my time incarcerated. I was forced to sneak my homework and study for exams inside of a state facility up until my release day. Needless to say, I made straight As and would later graduate cum laude with honors the same semester I was released, which I earned partially while imprisoned.

On the day I was released, I recall one of the correctional officers saying his farewell, which ended with, "We'll see you soon . . . You'll be back," to accompany the look of disgust my freedom truly brought him. I will never forget vowing to him and myself that I would never step foot in that facility or that county for the rest of my life. It's been over sixteen years since my release . . . I have yet to break that vow.

The week I was released just happened to coincide with my university's homecoming. It goes without saying that I relished every second of the festivities more than any of my peers that year. Two months later, I graduated cum laude with honors with my Bachelor of Business Administration degree, but my graduation was much more than the traditional celebration of an academic achievement. It was a momentous occasion that represented my reentry into society and my matriculation through my self-inflicted hardships. It served as a redemption-level event that I wouldn't have persevered through had it not been for my restored and renewed faith throughout those months of uncertainty and during my incarceration. My faith in myself to redeem and reclaim my life and future was unwavering and remains so to this day.

After over fifteen years, I now stand on the same faith that allowed me to walk across the stage to retrieve my bachelor's degree and my master's in business administration that I obtained three years after my release. I now reside in a metropolitan city and have made it to heights I never imagined I'd reach in my career, although the first few years on the road to reclamation were littered with challenges and potholes—if you ever been to Atlanta, you know I mean that literally. My faith, which may require a recharge and reboot from time to time, continues to carry me through and to peaks that I hadn't set my own sights on yet.

I now no longer carry the shame of my past or let it discourage me from opportunities for growth. I have refused to allow it to define and discount me as I let myself live in my present and release the past along with self-doubt, the thoughts of unworthiness, and the manufactured ideology of what an "ex-con" is and can be to society. I have taken the charge to rally behind causes to reduce recidivism and raise support for those who are preparing to return or have recently returned to society, and I actively seek to lead the charge in authoring a new narrative surrounding ex-offenders.

My hope is to allow my faith to become contagious and fuel a movement that will allow for life after incarceration to no longer be a lifelong sentence of disenfranchisement and dehumanization. I envision a society that embraces redemption and rejects prejudice toward those who have made poor decisions. A nation that doesn't allow for outright legal discrimination toward a class of citizens who are expecting to contribute just as their fellow citizens yet are impacted by the voices and votes of others with little to no say or representation.

My ambition to be the change I want to see has gifted me with a testimony that I feel compelled to share and has forced me to become more comfortable in my own skin. I now live with an abundance of gratitude and appreciation for being blessed with more than I could have envisioned the day the gavel was slammed on my future. I have my life, I have my health, I have a sound mind, I have a heart filled with determination, and, if nothing else, I have faith.

Romans 3:23–26

For all have sinned and fall short of the glory of God; being justified freely by His grace through the redemption that is in Christ Jesus: Whom God hath set forth to be a propitiation through faith in his blood, to declare his righteousness for the remission of sins that are past, through the forbearance of God; to declare, I say, at this time his righteousness: that he might be just, and the justifier of him which believeth in Jesus.

Carlos Scott, MBA

Chapter 2

UNPACKING BOXES

Something is wrong . . . Something is different. What is this? This strange feeling . . . What's happening to me? These thoughts, these growing concerns, sprung up into my mind as if they were antibodies primed to defend me against a foreign bacteria.

They became louder and louder in my mind as I attempted to force this sensation back down . . . Suddenly, the gravity of what I was in the midst of doing hit me. It was May 14, 2021, and I was an invited guest speaker for the historic Legendary Life Conference, hosted by *New York Times* bestseller Tommy Breedlove at the beautiful Atlanta Evergreen Marriott Conference Resort. Tommy, a passionate full-time speaker, life coach to the C-suite executive, and someone who fully embraced his calling to help others live their best and most legendary lives, presented the opportunity to be a featured speaker at his conference.

This is exactly what I wanted to do for so long. Now, I'd given talks to groups before, but this was different—submitting a professional headshot and a well-crafted professional bio different. I had been preparing for this moment for weeks, my big opportunity, in that room, at that moment, and I was experiencing something strange.

My mind leaped from the introspective task of diagnosing my condition and turned outward. The thought, *I don't have time for this; I'm a professional and I'm giving a talk*, snapped me out of that small disruption in an otherwise unobstructed flow of execution. Just like that, the tempo changed in my mind, and I quickly attempted to gain my composure. In these rare instances, I find that I often ground myself in the present moment, which allows my thoughts to become clear again. Sort of an emotional muscle memory, and it was very effective—well, usually, it was. I wondered where I learned . . . *Never mind that*. Almost instantly, I regained focus, and the sensation I was experiencing quickly faded into obscurity. I continued with my presentation.

A question . . . I was answering a question . . . What was it? My eyes wrestled back from the brink of concern. I focused on one of the men across the room, who was staring at me in anticipation of a response to his question. *Ah, yes, the question. He asked a simple question.*

Before I was interrupted by that mysterious internal jolt, the gentleman had asked, "Out of all the youth that you have worked with, how did you know who would make it and who wouldn't? Is there a way for you to tell?" He asked these very questions as a result of the talk I had just given about creating positive momentum in one's life. In this talk, I referred to my experience working with the underserved youth and how the unique lessons I gleaned from my work could be immensely effective in creating a better life for oneself.

"Great question!" I belted out in a confident and reassuring tone, reestablishing my flow. To me, this question was the perfect opportunity to end my speech on a strong note. Immediately, my mind began the process of crafting a well-worded and value-entrenched response; another gem of wisdom and insight was cooking. My brain immediately went to work, reaching into the vaulted depths of my experience to retrieve some gem of keen perspective to share with the audience eager from my response.

Then, something happened: A vivid picture popped into the forefront of my mind. It was as if I'd typed that question into a search engine, and almost immediately, a result pinged back with just as much casualness. It was a mental snapshot of Antonio. This was surprising because Antonio was someone I didn't even realize I had categorized away under the "Didn't Make It" category in my mind. However, there he was.

Mentally, this felt like I was looking for a very specific item in a room full of packed boxes, and I came across his box, opened it, and began to dig, in search of a reason as to why he didn't make it. Suddenly, I remembered everything about him. See, I worked with Antonio at a group home, where I was a house parent (essentially, a live-in care provider) at a group home facility.

I remembered doing everything from cooking and preparing meals (to the best of my ability at the time) to providing observation-based reports, giving medication, and offering solicited life advice to the young guys about a range of topics, from dealing with crushes and talking to girls, to navigating life. Essentially, I was like a hired big brother or parent for the young men in the group facility I worked for. Most don't know this, but group home facilities are scattered everywhere, in many different neighborhoods and communities.

Out of all the boys in that particular house, Antonio was the shortest, most opinionated, most confident, most resilient resident—definitely one of the peer leaders in the group home company I worked with at the time. In short (pun intended), although Antonio had a lot of mouth, he also had a lot of heart. I looked at him almost like an annoying little brother. However, as a result of his very spirited attributes, he would often find himself in conflict with not just some of the other residents in the home but the staff, as well. He would routinely let everyone in the home know that his respect wasn't to be given freely for any reason, regardless of if you were an adult, and had to be earned.

I know this to be true because I had it. However, if you didn't have it, he could be difficult to deal with, to say the least. See, the thing I remember the most about him was his passion for high school track and how he knew he was going to be famous for his talents. It was so infectious that everyone knew and believed in him and his abilities. I did, as well, to the point where I often would help him train by going on jogs with him up and down Marbut Road or in the neighborhood whenever I would come on my weekly shift. I definitely was not a jogger; however, he consistently bugged me to go on runs with him, often attempting to rush me through my work duties so I could.

Antonio would even heckle the other boys in the home for holding up our jogging sessions because they needed me for something. Then, once all my staff duties were finally completed and the residents were squared away, we would walk outside, stretch, and begin jogging through the neighborhood. On days when I didn't feel up to it, I remember hearing him antagonizing me with light insults about my weight, calling me old even though I was barely in my twenties, which he reminded me constantly was old to him, and telling me how jogging with him in the neighborhood would be mutually beneficial for us both. That it even could magically help me become more attractive to the ladies . . .

Antonio was killed by an accidental gunshot wound to the stomach. One of his friends was passing around a gun they found, and it discharged, hitting Antonio and killing him almost instantly. He was sixteen, and he was survived by his little brother and sister, both in group homes at the time. I attended his funeral. I don't even think I cried once about it then; probably just filed it away as another one who didn't make it.

As for the fame he always wanted and I actually believed he would achieve, they wrote about the incident in the paper and on a local news website . . . I'm certain that the two impassive paragraphs written about his untimely demise wouldn't equate too much in the way of fame. He deserved more. I did mention that he was in the "Didn't Make It" category, right? So, there was no answer to "The Question" to be found there.

However, before I could dismiss him from my mind, another box was opened and another mental picture was displayed. Just like before, all the details flooded back in, and just like before, the reason why they didn't make it didn't reveal itself, triggering another facial expression on my part. This "error" loop repeated itself in my mind a dozen times in mere seconds, all while I was giving the presentation. Suddenly, the uncomfortable sensation returned stronger and more determined for its presence to be acknowledged.

It was this dull pull from deep down, almost as if it was below me, behind me. Definitely a pain, but presented in a different way, almost like a pressure filling my body, working its way up. I stood there, faltering, not by the loaded question or even by the growingly aggressive pull I felt, but by an overwhelming highlight reel of—if I'm being honest—unprocessed trauma playing in my mind, sped up in 8K resolution. At that very moment, it was as if I had mentally walked into a room of "Didn't Make It," filled with towering boxes with names and faces attached. I hurriedly rushed in, looking for an answer, and disturbed one too many boxes.

They all started to come violently tumbling down and out of the room they were so carefully stored in. These boxes filled my mind and flooded out as tears. I remembered feeling myself subtly start to shake, my embarrassment being drowned out by shock and confusion. *What's wrong with me?* I asked myself, half-expecting an answer as my chest tightened and breathing became difficult. All the way up until that point, I had given a phenomenal presentation.

Every point immaculately delivered, every joke landed, every cue masterfully executed. I was simply crushing it. I could even confirm this because while I was speaking, I would occasionally glance over at the host, Tommy, whose facial expressions brandished this look of immense pride, with occasional moments of conformational head nodding each time I would share one of my proverbial gems of wisdom with the group.

Imagine a room of leaders, some of whom are heads of substantial organizations with tons of employees, many of whom have traveled to be there from as far as Ireland to attend this conference in personal development. At the height of my talk, I saw these gentlemen taking notes as if they were in a college core class with an inspired professor. I even hired the super talented fellow ASU Alum and world-class videographer AC Hampton to capture this extraordinary moment. I truly was experiencing a manifestation of what I believed to be my God-given purpose on this planet by giving this talk. However, I believe that in such moments, God takes the opportunity to show you things that you would have not been able to see otherwise.

At our highest and lowest moments, we are primed to receive truths. Because now, the silence in the room was deafening as I struggled for what seemed like an eternity to answer. To break the uncomfortable silence, I rescued a response from the grasp of what I could only describe as a breakdown. I began to answer the question.

"How could I know who's going to make it? Who's not? It's tricky, but what I think it comes down to is 'Patterns over potential,' or more precisely, 'Patterns are the prerequisite for reaching or realizing your greatest potential,' meaning that your ultimate potential is directly connected to your intentional and consistent actions. Regardless of how fervently you try or how passionately you wish to achieve, if your patterns do not align with your desired outcome, the likelihood of achieving success is greatly diminished. In my experience, most behavior patterns correlate with two distinct categories: a pattern of self-destruction or one of self-reparation. All that being said, for some, even surviving the process of growth can be seen as making it."

Well, this response was what I wished my logical brain, free from the emotions that arrested my moment, was able to generate at that time. However, God is so good because even in the midst of what I felt was an embarrassing situation, I still fulfilled my purpose of impact. After my presentation, I was approached by various members of the conference about what I had shared. Each felt compelled to share their struggles with everything from suicide to childhood neglect and trauma, all seeking my advice and embracing me as value added to the conference.

I still keep in contact with some of them to this day. I walked away from the experience feeling good. The irony is that I went into this opportunity thinking about the insight I was going to give, but in fact, I left receiving more. I knew I was shown this experience for the purpose of looking inward and doing the work on myself.

In order for me to truly impact others and function in my purpose, I must first unpack, process, then proceed. I think often as men, especially Black men, we are pressured to just skip to the last step and proceed. We'll tell ourselves whatever we need to get ourselves there or simply ignore the "it" into becoming a version of ourselves that is a constant state of "proceed." However, no matter how strong and "all right" we think we are or how unaffected we may appear to be, the truth is that there is no such thing as a free lunch. Everything has a cost.

Every experience, interaction, life event, or exchange leaves an impression on us. This wasn't new news to me. I always found myself mindful of the cost of my experiences. I guess what allowed me to achieve my static "proceed" state without ever really unpacking the most important boxes in my life was a saying I learned as a way to shift my perception during difficult times. The saying goes, "In life, things don't happen to you; they happen for you," meaning that every experience, good or bad, was an avenue for growth.

Although this saying is powerful and beneficial, I used this saying as a blanket to cover all of the "costs" of my challenging experiences like a credit card with a super high limit. The issue is that I didn't take the time to fully unpack and process potential traumas. I just shoved them into a box titled "Not to Me, but for Me" and chucked it into a back room full of other boxes.

That isn't it. If I am to live in my God-given purpose effectively and walk in my role as a man, father, husband, leader, etc., I must do the work and unpack my own experiences in a healthier way.

Then, I can move on to letting go of what no longer serves me and move forward. By not doing so, by not removing the plank in my own eye first like written in Matthew 7, how can I hope to have a positive impact in the lives of others? Every opportunity to have a positive impact and to walk into my purpose would be threatened to be hijacked otherwise.

IN ORDER TO MOVE FORWARD, I MUST DEAL WITH WHAT IS BEHIND ME.

Before I started writing my chapter, I prayed and asked God to guide me in addressing and unpacking my past experiences with the goal of moving in my purpose and encouraging others to do the same. So, I invite the person reading this—YES, YOU—to pray with me right now before moving on to my written words. Don't worry; you can pray this prayer no matter your religious status or beliefs. Here we go:

Thank You for my life. Thank You for my path. Thank You for every challenge I received. Please continue to grant me grace when I fail myself or land wide of the mark. Please continue to grant me the opportunity to matter in the lives of those around me and, most importantly, to myself. Thank You for continuing to guide me towards my life's purpose. Amen.

Unpacking the Start:

After that eye-opening experience speaking at that conference, I took a few days to process and figure out how I should proceed. Although I was receiving congratulations from those in my circle, I couldn't fully acknowledge the praise or fully answer when asked what happened. I decided to focus on why I was how I was, like what led to me being stuck in a static "proceed" state and not really acknowledging the weight of things I've experienced. However, up to this point, I haven't told you who I am.

So, allow me to introduce myself. My name is Stephen Churn, and I am the eldest son of Anthony and Phyllis Churn, older brother to Jonathan and Amber Churn. I was born and raised in Atlanta and Decatur, Georgia. I spoke about "my God-given purpose" earlier in my chapter, but I didn't clearly state it. I know that my purpose is and has always been to help others. It's not even something that I aspired to add to my life; it just was.

I noticed one day that people felt comfortable talking to me, and that often led to them telling me about their life. Even to complete strangers, I would start a casual conversation, and before I even realized it, they were sharing a trauma, a hidden personal insight about themselves, or a challenge they were navigating. I would ask a few questions, give my opinion, and bam! They would usually leave the exchange feeling better, with a renewed sense of direction.

Like most of us, this purpose was instilled in me by my parents. Both taught me a strong sense of community, responsibility, and to always do what you can to help others. My mother (the more extroverted parent) worked for DFACS (Department of Family and Child Services) and also as an executive director of a group home facility. I remember running up and down the halls of a shelter with my brother as a kid and hanging out with a lot of the kids in those homes, some of whom stayed with us for periods of time.

It always gave me an appreciation for those we call family. All of this was just normal—well, until middle school, when my mother started picking me and my brother up from school in front of all the other students in a white Ford Taurus with a big black Department of Family and Child Services crest on the side of the door. Yeah, that was fun. So, it shouldn't surprise anyone that my first job was working at a group home under my mother.

My father (the more introverted parent) was a property manager and maintenance technician for various properties including many of the apartment complexes we grew up in. He also was very active in the church as well as in the community. He was a very hard worker, and he taught me a lot about how to take care of a family. My father was the type of guy who could fix everything and could give you better directions than a GPS just from memory. Both of my parents were well-known and respected by many.

So, in order to unpack the start, I had to ask myself the "why"—or, to be more accurate, what was the root of how I started packing the boxes? The very first instance that I could remember started with my father and something I'd honestly forgotten I had experienced until this writing project. When I was very young, maybe six or seven, I remember my father receiving a phone call while we were all in the living room of our apartment.

Moments after he answered the phone, he began to break down, sobbing in a manner that, up until that point, I had never seen before. Unfortunately, he received news that his sister, my aunt Laytone, whom I knew very little at that point, had been killed in a gruesome manner, and her remains had been found. I can still clearly see the look of confusion on my little brother's face as we both stood there watching our father wrestle with waves of shock, grief, and pain of losing a family member in that manner.

I can still hear my little voice telling my father that everything was going to be okay as I attempted to console him the way a child does when they see something is wrong with their parents. What I remember next was a brief funeral with a closed casket, and shortly after that, my father went right back to work. I think something about my father going back to work and not taking the time that he probably should have to heal left an impression on me about how strong men operate. To this day, I am considered the strong friend's "strong friend," someone who remains calm and unshaken by what is happening, no matter how bad. This has allowed me to approach life differently and remain centered in most situations. To be clear, it is not a negative thing to be calm and centered in the midst of a crisis. In fact, many expert survival tips start with, "Try and remain calm." However, one thing I have realized is that just because you make it out of the crisis doesn't mean that the crisis has made it out of you.

Opportunity Is a Stage:

As we pulled into the parking lot of the Atlanta Job Corps campus, I looked at the surrounding neighborhood and observed the environment. I thought it was interesting to see the contrast between the older neighborhood which the Atlanta Job Corps is set in the middle of and all of these young students moving about on campus. Once we made it through the security gate and filed out of the work vehicle which we carpooled in, my coworkers and I lined up and approached the entrance of the building.

This would always naturally turn into an opportunity for the students we helped enroll into the program to speak to us as they went about their classes. I enjoyed this part because it allowed us to see the good work we'd been doing with helping students get into the program and change their lives. As I walked into the building, I watched all of my veteran coworkers who had spent more time in admissions speak to numerous students as they walked through the building.

At this point, because I was relatively new, I was seeking a familiar face so I could at least say hello, but that didn't happen until a little later in the day. While we were in the building, it felt like a field trip as we were escorted downstairs to an auditorium. This was my first time witnessing the thirty-day pep rally, so for those who don't know, part of our position was to not only get the students into the program successfully but to provide support for the students to matriculate all the way through the program, eventually landing into jobs or better circumstances. Because of this, we had metrics that we were responsible for, and we would get reports on the thirty-, sixty- and ninety-day results of our students remaining in the program.

This day was special because it was designed to not only incentivize the students to stay longer in the program but to signify that they'd made it to their thirty-day mark. As I walked through this building, I was told that the Atlanta campus is housed in the very first Black hotel in Atlanta. It held a significant level of importance to me to see these Black youth persevering and growing in an environment to better themselves.

However, when it came time for the pep rally to start, there was an issue. My manager, Charles Hill, told me that the keynote speaker did not show up. He then turned to me and asked if I would want to get up there and say a few words. He mainly did this because he had always joked and said that I could talk to even a wall and get the wall to talk back to me.

The reason he said this was because no matter where we went, I was always talking to people and making fast friends, and he was simply amazed that I was an extrovert who could establish connections with anybody. So, he would often test his theory. He would listen to me talk to students in my office and comment on how inspirational he thought that I was. However, this wasn't just in my office with one or two students but in this auditorium with over one hundred teens and young adults becoming impatient.

I looked at him and said, "All right. Sure. I'll do it." I mean, how hard could it be? So, I turned, walked up to the stage, and approached the microphone, and as I was doing so, the roar of idle chatter in the room became louder. I looked around the room and saw that everybody was preoccupied in conversation, so I introduced myself as an admissions counselor. Immediately, one of the students I had recently enrolled began to stand up and clap for me. She sat back down, and I could see her telling her friends that this was about to be good based on the session that we'd had when I got her enrolled into the program. She even pulled out her phone as if to prepare for a viral moment.

After I introduced myself, I told the students that I was there to say a few words to them. I told them that I would share a saying of mine that I tell my students often: You can't be the person you used to be and the person you want to be at the same time. "You can't be the person you used to be and the person you want to be at the same time," I repeated for the second time. I noticed something very strange was happening.

The distracting noise of idle conversation amongst the students in the audience almost immediately died down. I glanced up into the left at my student, whose face was gleaming with pride as she slowly covered it with her cell phone recording me talk. I glanced down and saw another young lady with this intense expression on her face, like she'd just heard the first impactful verse of her new favorite song as she shifted in her seat and leaned forward. Before I realized it, I had captured the attention of everybody in that room, and then I felt goosebumps on my skin as I spoke.

I told the students that regardless of where they were in their lives, by enrolling in this program and choosing to stay positive while they worked to better themselves, they were picking the best version of themselves. As I continued to talk, I could tell that I was operating in my purpose, even if it was for twenty to twenty-five minutes. For me, it was as simple as looking into the audience and speaking to what I could see. That's exactly what I did; it's what I always do. Looking at their collective faces, I could see the uncertainty of being in the new environment. I could see the doubt, the fear, the concern of "Am I going to mess this up again?", and other things. And I spoke to it, to all of it. Looking back, I realized that whenever I would talk to people, a portion of what I was saying was directed at myself.

After that experience, it was stapled that Churn had the gift of gab and the ability to make everybody feel good and comfortable when he spoke to them. Or, at least, that's what my manager and coworkers shared about me to everybody else in and outside the office. And although I acknowledge that is a blessing and something that makes me feel good to hear others refer to me as, looking back, I can see how it had a hidden cost to it.

Every Thursday, we had something called an orientation. An orientation was when new potential students would come into the office, and one of our team members would speak to them about the program, answer questions, and inspire them to take the next step for themselves. We each had different days to do this, and it directly affected our roster of students we could get into the program. Each student was a part of our success metric, and having students not only enroll in but complete the program could result in a bonus.

For me, orientation was an opportunity for me to talk to groups, and in the back of my mind, I felt like that was the perfect training ground for me to speak to strangers and attempt to inspire them. After the orientation, we would schedule one-on-one meetings, and this is where making everyone comfortable had its hidden cost: The more comfortable people feel with you, the more they share. What they share could cost you more than you think.

As a part of my job, I had to learn a little bit about each individual that sat in front of me and make the assessment of if they would be successful in the program. I had other coworkers who were way more efficient in their assessments, extracting the bare minimum of information they needed to complete students' applications and get them into the program. Admittedly, I had moments where I did this, as well, in order to take a shot at a bonus that month, but more than often, I found myself learning about the students' motivations and backstories and all the things that got them to that point.

In those one-on-one interviews, you quickly learned that they were not for the weak at heart. One of my favorite coworkers, Tracy, would keep tissues on her desk because her one-on-one interviews were notorious for the potential students crying during them. By the end, they would see Tracy as more of a loving auntie and would do what they could to complete the program successfully.

As for me, my interviews usually went from therapy sessions to comedy sessions to motivational talk to getting them into the program. For the potential students who didn't qualify, some would come back to the office just to talk to me and give me updates on their lives. I enjoyed the interactions with and stories from all of the applicants. During those one-on-ones, I learned so much more than the students, the community, and even the human condition as a whole. I learned more about myself.

When we are put into different circumstances, we often see different sides of ourselves. I was impressed with the amount of empathy I could show to a stranger without pitying them. I gave every student who walked into my office a large amount of grace that they couldn't seem to give themselves. This allowed me enough time to figure out what was holding them back and to speak to it as something they could overcome. This was not as easy as I'm making it sound, and the most challenging situations would often come out of nowhere. A young lady with the bright red glasses is a perfect example of that.

I had a young lady come into my office for a one-on-one, and as you guessed it, she had these bright red frames. She was a small, dark-skinned, soft-spoken young woman with a very bright smile. She initially seemed sort of nervous but had this bubbly personality. As we were going through the course of the interview, I could tell she became comfortable talking to me. Immediately, she seemed like a very good candidate for the program and had all of the motivation, I believed, to complete it successfully.

At this point in the interview, I had already made the determination to put her in the program, and so everything was just casual conversation while we completed the paperwork. We cracked a few jokes, and I gave her a compliment about her glasses to which she replied she took great pride in her style. I asked her if she was always such a positive person, and she said she tried to be, even when dealing with certain things. So, I asked, "Like what?", and she told me that a couple of nights ago, her brother, who was recently released from prison, had a big celebration. He came home drunk and sexually assaulted her . . . She said this to me with a conversational tone that did not match what she had just told me.

It took me about half a second to register what she said while I was flipping back and forth through her application. When it finally hit me, I quietly looked up at her, and what I thought was initially nervousness suddenly revealed itself to be her struggling to keep herself together. I believe she did it so she could finish the interview and get into the program . . . In that moment, my heart broke for her. It broke for all the young women and young people in our community who experience unimaginable situations.

We both were quiet for a few seconds . . . I looked at her, and she kept her same composure. I took a deep breath and said, "That's terrible . . . I'm so sorry that happened to you." In moments like that, there's no quote or saying anyone can provide. The only thing I could think to do was to keep my composure, as well, although I wanted to reach around the table and hug her. I knew if I broke down, she would, too. I could see she wasn't going to let anything stop her from completing her mission.

Making it into the program, which provided residence for the students allowing them to escape their environment, was what she felt she needed. More words were exchanged, and at the end of our conversation, I told her that I would do whatever I needed to do to help her, and she thanked me. About two months later, I was at the Atlanta campus, where I gave the talk I spoke about earlier.

As I was leaving the campus, something bright red caught my eye. It was her, with her bright red frames, laughing and smiling with a group of friends. She looked completely different from the day of our interview. She looked full and happy. I think God puts us in places for a reason, and we are fortunate to see the reason unfold—and if we are very lucky, we get to see the contribution on our part.

I find myself often looking for reason and purpose in every situation, challenge, gain, or loss. It all happens to shape us in some way, which, in turn, potentially helps us shape those around us. This is something that is easy to understand in foresight, but honestly, while things are happening to us in real time, it's extremely difficult to grasp.

During my four years working in that position at Job Corps, I experienced some of the most impactful moments of my adult life and many highs and lows. For example, I received the call that my little brother was going to prison, and I sat in my office, heartbroken. I remember fighting back tears with my door closed, and I thank God I had the sense to get up and walk across the hall to my coworker, Tracy (rest in peace).

Tracy was able to show me compassion and allowed me to make it through the rest of the day. That instance reminded me that God places people around you to help you process and unpack, to help you grow into the version of yourself who walks in your purpose. But it is up to us to engage, receive, and be brave enough to allow that process to take place. Looking further back, I can think about challenging situations that I didn't share with anyone else because . . . well, I don't know.

Now, I know that we have to intentionally face the things that are stored inside of us and utilize tools like prayer and even therapy to free ourselves from some of the things that continue to hold us. Even the process of writing this chapter has shaken loose from things that I seldom think about but could feel the weight of on my heart. I'm not sure if we bury challenging life situations in order to continue to function as we think we should.

Maybe we do so because those difficult times are attached to our insecurities, and acknowledging that we struggled or are struggling is acknowledging that we are less than in our own eyes and the perceived eyes of others. However, I know that God's purpose for us is definitely not for us to battle with our difficulties in isolation. We always can pray and seek resolution through not only the word but through the resources that He has placed in our lives around us. We have to not only acknowledge the lessons but embrace them.

I thank you and everyone for taking the time to read my chapter, and it is my hope that you take inventory of the unpacked boxes in your life. That you intentionally take steps to unpack and process the experiences that have been bestowed upon you. By doing so, you make way for the blessing of growth. I also want to take a moment and thank my friends and family for the support they have graciously given me through this process. Speaking of the process, I must take time to thank Toni and Riel, the BFF Publishing team, for the enormous amount of work you ladies have done on our behalf.

Most importantly, I want to understand that this is a journey, and life doesn't stop. Even while writing my chapter, I, like the other authors in the book, experienced all manner of challenges. However, we made it! Hopefully, the stories contained in these chapters encourage you to make it, as well.

Stephen Churn

Chapter 3

Family Matters

The worst moment in my life was when I woke up in the hospital unaware of my whereabouts or how I got there. The first thing I recall about that moment was me awakening from what seemed like a long sleep and a nurse asking me if I knew where I was. I told the nurse no. The nurse told me that I was in the M.E.D. I did not know what the M.E.D. was at the time. She told me that I was in the hospital in Memphis, Tennessee. She explained that I was paralyzed from the neck down due to a terrible car accident.

I did not believe her and was not aware of the numerous tubes throughout my entire body. I told her angrily that I was not paralyzed from the neck down and that my truck was outside. I immediately tried to get up so I could go to my truck to leave and go home. However, I could not move anything but my eyeballs. At that moment, I knew the nurse was telling the truth. I knew something horrendous had happened because I could not move any of my limbs. Although I wished I was dead, I could not commit suicide because I could not move any of my limbs to do so. Therefore, I could only lie in my tears and think, *How did I end up here?*

Throughout childhood, I was angry. I was a daddy's boy as far back as I can remember. I used to love country life. Between the ages of two and seven, my dad spent time with me and showed me love. My dad participated in outdoor activities with me, including riding my big wheel and taking me fishing. I thought my mom, dad, sister, and I were one big family—until we were not anymore.

My parents separated when I was four years old and divorced when I was seven years old. My dad slowly stopped spending time with me and showing me the love that I was accustomed to. I constantly asked my mom where my dad was. I missed my dad. I wanted to spend time with my dad. My mom grew extremely tired of me throwing temper tantrums about my dad's whereabouts. Once I was much older, she told me that she'd tried saying and doing anything to make me hush and stop acting out. She went to the extreme and told me that my father was dead to make me stop throwing temper tantrums. My mom's decision was ineffective. I still missed my dad and had crying spells about it.

In addition, I became an angry child. I had to temporarily stay at numerous aunts' and uncles' homes on my dad's side of the family in the country while my mother worked two jobs to support me and my sister. Each household I had to stay at included a wife, a husband, and children. I had fun at the homes because I was around family, and I enjoyed the country life.

However, I still missed my dad because he was working out of town and still making more children but not spending enough time with me. Each time I stayed at one of my aunts' and uncles' homes, it triggered my anger. I would overthink about where my dad was and why my family could not stay together. I lived in my head by thinking and wishing my parents got back together.

The temporary moves transitioned into permanent moves. I had become a mother's boy. No one could separate me from my mother. It seemed like I had lost one parent, and I did not want to lose another. I did not want to leave my mother's sight. I hated when she went to work and left me at her parents' home in town, although my grandfather, L.C. Smith, was my guardian angel.

My grandmother did not like me because I looked like my dad. My grandmother despised my dad, and every time I was around her, she showed me that she disliked me as a result of it. She eventually manipulated my mom into forcing me to permanently move in with my Uncle Harvey and Aunt Linda Mitchell, along with their two sons, Amaud and Antonio Mitchell. My grandmother was easily able to manipulate my mom by telling her a little bit of the truth, which was that my mother's side of the family included mostly girls. My grandmother told my mother when I was seven years old that I needed to move in with my Uncle Harvey and Aunt Linda because they had boys. She insisted that I did not need to be around all the girls in the family.

My mother forced me to move away from her and my sister to live with my Uncle Harvey and Aunt Linda far out in the country. Although I loved my Uncle Harvey, Aunt Linda, Amaud (Shaud), and Antonio (Tony), I did not want to separate from my mother and sister. I felt so angry because I could not live with my own family. Although I knew my mother loved me and took great care of me, I did not feel loved by her decision. I felt like a thrown-away child.

I later embraced the move with my Uncle Harvey and Aunt Linda. They played a significant role in the man I have become today. My uncle became a father to me. He taught me how to grow up and be a man. He spent time with me and showed me love, although it was tough love. He took me fishing, to play pool, and to play basketball, and he made sure I got up to attend Sunday school and church service every Sunday morning. He supported me by attending my football games in junior high school and high school when not too many others did.

He taught me how to be independent and disciplined. He taught me how to drive, complete chores, do yard work, and work on cars. He was also a disciplinarian. When I did something wrong at home or school, he pulled me to the side and had significant talks with me that I did not appreciate enough at the time. He was trying to provide structure and guidance, but I was too hardheaded to understand during the ages of seven to eleven.

For example, my uncle saw a hickey on my neck. He had me join him outside on the back porch to discuss it. I was scared and chose to lie. I told him it was a rash. He immediately told me he was not born last night, and he knew what it was. I could not tell him what it was because I knew he would start asking me questions about who, when, and where. I could not tell him it was from Jessica Rabbit, whom he was very close to. She was about five or six years older than me. I could not tell him she had been showing me how to touch and kiss—and later, to penetrate—since I was around seven years old.

My Aunt Linda played a significant role with teaching me about God, self-worth, and education. For instance, she always preached to me about knowing my worth and not settling for less. She placed in my heart at a young age the desire to want to attend college when I got older. She made sure I was involved in activities, including Boy Scouts and karate. She took me camping and taught me how to survive in the wilderness, including setting up a tent and cooking over a campfire.

She was also a disciplinarian. She started off giving me whoopings when I did something wrong until she saw that whoopings were ineffective with me. I would sit there as she hit me as hard as she could, and I was not bothered by it. Once you have had a whooping by my mom, no other whoopings will bother you. Therefore, my aunt started making me do extra schoolwork when I got into trouble, which made me angry because I would miss a lot of Saturday cartoons or outdoor activities. But I'll say, I became pretty smart due to her method.

I loved living with my two cousins (brothers), Shaud and Tony. Shaud was about three years older than me, and Tony was one year younger than me. I did not feel alone and enjoyed spending time with them. I was happy to have two brothers whom I could talk to and have fun with. We did everything together, including eating as a family at the dinner table. We played basketball, football, kickball, and baseball together.

We went camping and participated in karate together. The karate instructors gave us the nickname, "3 Ninjas," from the movie *3 Ninjas*. We also imitated the Ninja Turtles. We each had a name and weapon. I was imitating Donatello, and I had a bo staff like him. I grew to love fighting, which was not good for a child who was masking his hurt and anger daily.

Although I loved living with my Uncle Harvey and Aunt Linda, I could not appreciate my blessings enough throughout childhood. I still missed my parents and sister. I did not get to spend enough time with them. Then, I wanted less structure and more fun with girls and my friends from school. Most of the girls and my friends lived in town and not far out in the country.

Jessica Rabbit, who taught me everything about how to please a girl from the ages of seven to twelve years old, contributed to my strong desire to spend time with girls and have sex at a young age. There were not many girls near my uncle and aunt's home, and sex or sexual behaviors stopped when I was about eleven or twelve years old when my aunt caught Jessica Rabbit riding me. My aunt blamed me, saying, "This is not a whore house." My aunt and mother always called me mannish, but they never knew why. They always blamed it on me having my father's whorish ways. They never knew what had been going on under everyone's noses since around seven years old.

With the above information in mind, I permanently moved with my aunt, Patricia Smith (Trish), in town—or what some people considered the hood or ghetto—at eleven years old. As a child, I thought I was making a good decision by leaving a household with structure to live in a less structured household. Trish was a single mother with three children: Kenyatta Smith (Nuky; one year older than me), Javeda Sikes (Veda; same age as me), and Jabari Smith (Dude; at least five years younger than me). She was the fun aunt. I loved living with Trish. I had more freedom to do whatever I wanted because she was at work most of the time. One of her few rules was not to have too many people in her house while she was gone, which I consistently broke. I enjoyed spending time with more people. I spent more time with my mother, sister, cousins, friends, and girls. However, I still visited my Uncle Harvey, Aunt Linda, Shaud, and Tony on some weekends.

Additionally, a plethora of bad decisions came with having more freedom at eleven years old. I was introduced to marijuana, alcohol, gangs, and selling drugs. I was fascinated by watching the reputation and material things drug dealers had, including cars, clothes, shoes, jewelry, and girls. They were well-respected in the environment I moved to. I wanted to be respected and to have the reputation and material things they had.

I started adopting the same behaviors. I started abusing marijuana and alcohol. I started having sex with as many girls as I could and as many times as I could daily. I started selling a lot of drugs. Curious George, who was a Vice Lord, taught me everything about making and selling crack before he trusted me on my own. I recall the first time I sold crack at night by myself. It was like a horror movie or Michael Jackson's "Thriller" video. The two guys I sold crack to looked like zombies as they feigned for crack. They were so anxious, whereas I was so nervous.

Selling crack became easier each time I sold it. I became confident and started strategizing how to sell more drugs. I was always smart; although, I did not use my intelligence for the right things throughout my childhood. For instance, I cut a hole in the inside of my 49ers Starter coat to hide my drugs and sometimes a gun from adults or authority figures. I slacked going on the corners to sell drugs where there was more competition from the opposite gang and less money.

I started waiting until functional crackheads got paid and had gatherings. I would go to their homes and sell everything I had. I had to go get more drugs, empty my pockets from all the money gained, and return to their homes to make more money. I made so much money. I was not smart enough to keep a lot of it. I mostly gave it to Curious George. He would give me some of the money to buy shoes, clothes, food, marijuana, and alcohol, to name a few things. He also taught me to get someone I could trust to sell drugs with me to make more money of my own. One of my best friends, Shotgun Shun, joined me to sell drugs. We made a lot of money together and enjoyed being able to get what we wanted. We became like brothers.

Moreover, gang activities started to increase between the ages of twelve and sixteen. A few friends and I started another branch called Freaky Ass Niggas (F.A.N.). Our main objective was to have fun and have as much sex with as many girls as possible. F.A.N. was created because the girls I'd respected ended up showing me the least interest or cheating on me. However, the girls I had sex with treated me with love and respect. Therefore, I lost respect for girls because I wanted to treat them like queens and not sex objects but was forced into becoming a savage. I gave them exactly what they wanted.

Additionally, my friends gave me the nickname Psycho because I behaved like I did not care and would fight anyone despite how tall or big they were. I had no fear of anything or anyone. My nickname changed from Psycho to Psycho Drama, and then from Psycho Drama to Drama. I started behaving the total opposite of everything my mother, Uncle Harvey, and Aunt Linda taught me. Most of my closest friends were Vice Lords except for Shotgun Shun. I hung around them daily.

They became my substitute family, my brothers. They were going through similar circumstances as me, including not having an active father in their lives. Most of their fathers were in jail or prison. I slowly stopped going to church because I chose to stay out all night on Saturdays doing gang activities or having what I thought was fun at the time. Every Sunday morning, when my mother would come to Trish's house to wake me up and take me to church, I would tell her that I would go next Sunday. This resulted in me seldomly going to church, if at all. The moment I opened my eyes, it was time to get in the streets. I would smoke marijuana outside at school before the bell rang to enter the school. I would skip classes to smoke more marijuana and have sex with girls. I started to fight often, especially at school, to relieve anger and hurt.

The multiple fights prevented me from playing football in the seventh grade; the school administrators would not allow the coaches to let me play football until the eighth grade because I got into trouble at school at least three times daily. I got into trouble mostly for fighting or because teachers refused to call me Sir or Sir Allen. They wanted to call me Allen, which I had zero tolerance for.

Moreover, fighting increased at school and in the streets as I entered high school. I could not be touched at school because I played football. I was feeling myself, and most would call me cocky, but I called it confidence. I was known as a ladies' man but welcomed fighting without fear. However, there was always drama with girls' boyfriends. I was fighting guys because they thought I was trying to steal their girls, but it was their girls who were constantly trying to talk to me and have sex with me. I would fight them for the hell of it, and I would take their girl even if I did not want her just to show the guys I was not to be messed with.

I always had good in me. My anger and hurt just did not allow me to show the good unless I was around certain people. I just wanted to have fun and love people. I was trying to change when I met a special girl, Cinderella. She was a senior in high school, and I was a freshman. Everyone tried to get into a relationship with her, but they could not. Most guys called her stuck-up. Her type of guy was the total opposite of me. She did not like a guy who cursed, smoked, drank, and was loud, to name a few traits. I had a Spanish class with her. Most of my friends were kicked out of school or skipped school. I would go to sleep daily in that class.

One day, she woke me up and spoke. I spoke and tried to go back to sleep, but she wanted to talk. I wanted a relationship with her. Everyone told me I could not get with her because no one had any luck except for the star running back. I accepted the challenge. I stopped smoking in the bathrooms at school. I started meeting her at the library after school, a place I'd never been inside of prior to her wanting to meet there. I'd also go there to help my cousin Playboy because he was seeing her younger sister.

We grew closer. One night, I called her, and she told me she was ready to get into a relationship with me. I was elated. I started changing for the better to make her happy. I slacked on, if not stopped, doing everything I was doing wrongfully, including having sex and fighting. I was starting to be like the child my mother, Uncle Harvey, and Aunt Linda raised me to be.

I had to make a choice to continue to play football as a cornerback in the tenth grade or quit football to participate in more gang activities. I did not listen to Playboy, and I chose the latter like a fool but vowed to return as a senior in high school. I loved football. Football was my life. It was my stress reliever. I liked to hit people and have fun on the football field to relieve anger.

However, my anger towards my dad when hearing him say, "That's my son!" when playing football or someone talking about football but not saying it or showing me any other time contributed to my decision to quit football. I wanted him to show me love without football. I still missed my dad and did not want to give him the satisfaction of saying, "That's my son!" again unless it was outside of football.

Now, I did not have football as a coping skill, and my anger increased. My anger was uncontrollable. I stayed getting into it with a certain set of gangsters at school and in the streets. We fought at school and made plans to fight in the streets after school.

On the other hand, I thought I was invincible. No one, nothing, could touch us. In my Martin Lawrence voice, "Somebody done told you wrong." I was sadly mistaken. It was during the weekend of Shaud and Stallion's high school graduation (Stallion is one of my childhood friends and a member of F.A.N.). My friends and I were smoking and drinking the entire day. Tony the Tiger's younger brother had bought a car with crack.

I did not know it was God at the time, but I kept hearing a voice telling me not to get in that car the entire day. I told Stallion that I was not getting in the car because something was going to happen to them due to them driving recklessly. As the night grew later, my mother told me to go into the house. I went into the house like she told me to do, but later, I was disobedient by sneaking back out. It was around midnight when Stallion and I became bored.

I was planning to walk him halfway home just in case someone wanted to sneak up on us to fight. However, before we could leave the parking lot, Tony the Tiger pulled up and asked me and Stallion if we wanted to go to the store with him. We immediately looked at each other. We knew what we talked about prior to this conversation about not getting into the car. He pleaded with us, promising he would drive safely. We got into the car and went to the store. Tony the Tiger had driven safely.

He asked us if we wanted to ride with him to go to a party near Pegues Circle. We told him no. However, he persuaded us by telling us there would be a lot of girls there. We looked at each other and got into the car. Then, we picked up Freak Nasty to go to the party. I did not remember anything about the party. I was told by multiple people that there was a girl there that everyone was trying to get but did not succeed. I was able to get with her and left with her for a long time before my three friends and I left the party to go home.

It was raining on the way home. A car was on our side of the road with its lights on bright. Tony the Tiger swerved and wrestled with the car as we were aiming toward a tree. Stallion was in the front on the passenger side. He was asleep. He woke up and grabbed the wheel as we started heading toward the tree. Tony the Tiger jumped out of the car and climbed the tree, and leaving us to die as we slammed into it.

The car was in two pieces with only the trunk left as the car was wrapped around the tree. I was thrown out of the car from the back passenger seat. Part of the door's frame cut me as I was thrown out. If I had worn my seatbelt, the frame of the door that cut me would have gone straight through my chest. I was immediately paralyzed from the neck down.

I was screaming as I moved only my eyes to examine my body. I was bleeding significantly. My spine was broken. My left wrist was crushed, and my bone was sticking out. My head had burst open to where you could see my brain. As I was screaming, I heard another voice screaming in pain. It was Stallion with the motor pressed against his chest. As we looked into each other's eyes, I died. As my eyes closed, I could only see red. I do not know if it was because of all the blood I saw, or if I was actually in hell.

In addition, I did not remember being rejuvenated on a helicopter ride to the M.E.D. (Medical Emergency Department). My mom explained to me later that she was in disbelief when the doctors called her and told her to get to the M.E.D. because I was involved in a horrible car accident. My mother expressed to me later that she went through an emotional rollercoaster as the doctors called her at least three times before she left her home.

She said the doctors told her that I had died. She cried before the doctor called her again, stating that they'd revived me. She was happy. Then, she became extremely sad when the doctor called her again and told her they had lost me and to prepare to witness my body and plan for the funeral. She explained that the doctor called her one last time and told her that they had revived me once and for all, and I was stable. She expressed her gratitude to God when the doctors told her they did not know how I kept coming back to life. She explained that she and my loved ones rushed to the hospital to see me despite me being in a medically induced coma.

She told me the story of how Vice Lords came to the hospital to see me while I was in the coma. She explained that everyone had on red and had flags. Security guards surrounded my room because the staff at the hospital thought the Vice Lords were coming to kill me. My mother explained that she told them they were my friends before they allowed them to see me.

Moreover, I was in a medically induced coma for a month. My mother explained to me once I woke up and was stable that every patient in the ICU on the same floor as me died. She'd anointed the frame of the door in the room I was in and prayed, and death skipped me. Although I was heavily sedated and asleep, I still can recall the doctors taking me to have metal rods placed on each side of my spine.

On the way to have surgery, a doctor asked my mom if he could pray for me, and she allowed him to. After he finished praying for me, he told my mom not to worry about me because I was special. He told my mom that God had a calling on my life, a lot of work for me to do for Him, and I was not going to die. I heard everything in my sleep, but I never mentioned it until a few years later.

Additionally, awakening in a place of the unknown was scary, but there was nothing I could do about it because I had discovered I was paralyzed from the neck down. I was in so much pain. Most of my bones were broken, including my spine and ribs. I could barely breathe due to my ribs puncturing my lungs. I was always filled with morphine in an attempt to help reduce the pain. I was happy to see my family and true friends coming to visit me. I was not alone.

They showed me how much they loved and cared for me. They helped me change my focus from the pain to the fact that I had support, despite my anger about being in the worst condition of my life. My mother and my stepfather, TJ Coffey, visited me daily. I was always happy to see my mother. She was my comforter. She always spoke encouraging words when I was speaking negatively and wanting to die. Although she was in my room daily, it did not prevent her from visiting and praying for other patients in the ICU.

Moreover, I started to get a flinch in my fingers. I told and showed the nurse. The doctor gave me a robotic hand to help me learn to move my fingers again. My younger cousins were scared to come into the room when I had the robotic hands on because it reminded them of Freddie Krueger from the horror movies. I slowly started to regain feeling and movement in my upper body. The pain throughout my body increased. The doctor gave me easy access to morphine by allowing me to squeeze a pump that released morphine from an IV into my body. I slept most of the day if I wasn't in therapy.

I was driven by anger to go hard in therapy. I wanted to kill Tony the Tiger for jumping out of the car and leaving us to die. My entire focus in therapy was to strengthen my fingers and hands so I could hold a gun and pull the trigger to make Tony the Tiger feel the pain I felt in the hospital for at least *seventy-two days*. Seventy-two days was a long time not going outside and seeing the sun. My Aunt Linda was the first person to take me outside prior to being discharged from the hospital. I remember feeling like I was blind immediately when I went outside. I could not stay outside for more than one minute because the sun was too bright from staying inside for so long.

In addition, I was released from the hospital after missing the entire summer. I was taken back to my Uncle Harvey and Aunt Linda's home because their home was more wheelchair-friendly than my mother's home at the time of my release from the hospital. I was very grateful for them to help take care of me. I was on bed rest for at least another twenty-three weeks. I was missing the beginning of my eleventh-grade year.

I was strongly considering dropping out of school, thinking that I would only return if God got me up and let me walk again. However, family and friends encouraged me to go back to school. Partee, my Mississippi barber and friend, spoke the final words of encouragement that finally made me reconsider going back to high school. He told me that the world was going to go on with me or without me. He stated that my sister and my cousins were going to catch me and graduate before me if I did not return to school. The competitiveness kicked in, and I returned to school.

It was hell returning to school in the beginning. I had to catch up with all the work I had missed and complete the current assignments. I feared how others would look at me because I had a body brace on my upper body and a cast on my left arm, and I could not do much of anything for myself. However, family and friends, including Vice Lords and F.A.N., helped me get to my classes and to the restroom. I was always in pain. Vice Lords and F.A.N. protected anyone from getting in my way or touching me as they pushed me to my classes.

They would surround me as we went down the hall. I felt bad for anyone who got in the way or touched me. For instance, one boy did not get out of the way and mistakenly bumped my feet. Vice Lords and F.A.N. beat him down pretty bad. I felt guilty at first until I realized I was the same dangerous person I was prior to the car accident and had the same power if not more in the wheelchair. The power went to my head.

On the other hand, I eventually moved to my mother's home, far away from my family and friends, as I became stronger and more able to perform personal tasks daily on my own. When I was not at school, I was angry and showed it in the worst ways. I would break all my karate and football trophies and plaques. I would punch on my punching bag for hours without gloves until my knuckles no longer had skin on them. The meat of my knuckles showed and dripped blood as I continued to punch the bag.

I excessively smoked marijuana and drank alcohol that I could not take pressure breaks to relieve pressure off of my buttocks. I constantly talked negatively about why God allowed me to stay in this condition and my desire to die. My mother did not like being around me much because she called me crazy. She would cook for me in the afternoon and leave me at the house alone for the rest of the day. I told myself one night that I would have my final meal the next day. My mother cooked a hamburger and homemade french fries.

I waited until she left the house. I poured all of my pain pills on top of my burger. I was ready to die due to the mental and physical pain I dealt with daily. I was about to take a big bite of the burger, and I heard God's voice clearly tell me, "You are not going to die." I immediately dropped my food onto the plate, sat it aside, and cried hysterically. Here I was, so close to death, but God would not allow me to die. God continued talking to me. He told me if I wanted to be delivered from the pain and the wheelchair, I had to do it through Him. God started calling me to preach His holy word.

Although I wanted to stop hurting and to walk, I did not want to accept God's calling. I did not want to change my bad habits. I wanted to continue to smoke marijuana and have sex because those two things helped me block out the million negative thoughts and pain I dealt with every day. I told God no. I talked with my mother about my encounters with God, and I told her that I'd heard the doctor in the hospital telling her I was special and God wanted me to preach. I told her I told God no. My mother called me crazy and explained the danger I could be in for telling God no. I did not care. My life seemed over at the time, anyway.

Although I tried running from God's calling from 1999 to 2003, I slowly was trying to see if I could live righteously. I had mostly told God no because I did not want to be a hypocrite. I did not want to accept God's calling when I knew I was not ready to give up my sinful lifestyle. However, I slowly started trying harder to change for the better. I stopped everything pretty easily except for having sex. Sex was my number one drug. I stopped spending time with females alone. I isolated myself until I thought I was strong enough to allow a female to spend time with me alone. I failed every time. I could not tell a female no. It was my pleasure to please them.

I knew that I had to start making better decisions to prevent myself from having sex because God would not allow me to sleep the more I tried to run from Him. I knew I was ready in 2003 to accept God's calling when I told a female no for the first time. After I told her no about three times, she put my hand on her thighs and asked me if I was sure I did not want to have sex with her. My hand seemed like it melted into her thigh because it was so soft.

It hurt me to my soul to say no one last time, but the God in me helped me say no. I was not driving at the time, so I called my mother and told her I was ready to go home. She wondered why I was looking sad. I turned my head away from my mother and cried on the way home. My tears were bittersweet. It hurt me to say no, but it was sweet that I finally was ready to accept God's calling.

In 2003, two years after I graduated high school, my mother encouraged me to go to the University of Mississippi (Ole Miss) to pursue a bachelor's degree. She knew I wanted to attend college because my Aunt Linda had always emphasized the importance of getting a college degree. My mother knew I would not put my ego or pride to the side to ask her because I had already taken her through enough. I did not want to be a burden to ask my mother for her help because I was not 100% independent. I was happy and grateful that she asked me about attending college. I enrolled at Ole Miss in the summer of 2003 and accepted God's calling to preach in October 2003.

Although I was happy to attend Ole Miss and to start preaching God's word, Satan came after me harder. Satan was displeased with losing a soldier. I was no longer intentionally living in sin. Satan continued to attack my mind and body. Satan would put significant negative thoughts in my mind by telling me to give up after I would have trouble holding my bowels at Ole Miss. I can recall leaving the classroom before anyone could smell me and calling my mother to explain to her what happened and that I needed her help. Some days, Satan got the best of me by contributing to me leaving and not attending any more classes.

It was difficult to return to class after I was mentally devastated. I grew stronger with God and did not allow those same incidents to continue to make me leave school or miss any classes. I received help from my mother, prayed, rebuked Satan, and returned to class to show Satan that his tricks and attempts to take over my mind would no longer work in his favor. If anything, the incidents made me hate Satan even more. I was extremely grateful that my grandfather and other family members taught me the power of prayer.

Moreover, I graduated from Ole Miss with a bachelor's degree in psychology in 2007. It was difficult to find a job. I wanted to pursue a master's degree, but I was not about to be another burden on my mother. I wanted her to live her life. I was content with dealing with the cards I was dealt. However, my mother asked me yet again about furthering my college career. I was grateful for my mother coming to me and telling me she would help me attend a master's program. I accepted her help and attended Delta State University in 2009. Similar to when I attended Ole Miss, Satan continued to attack my mind and body. However, he started attacking my mind and body in different ways.

I got married in 2010. Delta State University was a two-hour commute from my wife's house. My wife and I separated quickly. Although I did not believe in a divorce, I was left with no other choice but to file for a divorce and get a place of my own. Satan tried to get me to give up on furthering my college career after my remaining two grandparents died, including my grandfather, L.C. I had surgery to remove a kidney stone shortly afterward. I had challenges with one professor not wanting to call me by my first name, Sir. Despite Satan's attempts, I pushed through and graduated with a 4.0 GPA in school and community counseling in May 2011.

Although I had a master's degree, I still faced many challenges to land a job. I would always make it to the final two interviewees but not get the job. It was heartbreaking that I had a master's degree but could not get a job and still was only drawing a disability check and financial help from family and friends. I was becoming depressed again due to financial issues.

One night, I was feeling depressed and defeated as I lay in my one-bedroom apartment in Batesville, Mississippi. I had reached my breaking point. I cried out and prayed extremely hard that night about needing God's help to fix my financial issues and to guide me the way He wanted me to go because I was stuck and did not know what else to do but pray. I prayed until I fell asleep. I woke up that morning, and God told me to move. I had no clue where to move. I always was a die-hard 49ers fan, and Shaud and Tony were living in California. I was thinking I could move to California. However, God directed me to move to Atlanta, Georgia.

I revealed to my family that God wanted me to move to Atlanta. Everyone knew how close I was to my mother and knew I still needed her help. They all told me that I was not moving away from my mother. However, a week later, I had scheduled to review some apartments in Atlanta. My Aunt Linda had volunteered to take me to get an apartment in Georgia. I did not know at the time that she had eye surgery the day before we were leaving to go to Atlanta.

I did not have any money to get to Atlanta because I had recently paid rent and other bills on a fixed income. I had to borrow money from a former professor, whom my family and I became close friends with. Mrs. Mari Kuhnle and her family are like family to me. Mrs. Kuhnle has always been supportive of me, which I greatly appreciate.

I soon discovered that my Aunt Linda could not see much, if at all. Although it was the scariest drive I have been on since the car accident that left me paralyzed, my Aunt Linda was determined to help me get to Atlanta. She could not see when to stop or turn. I had to tell her for more than six hours when to stop behind a car, to stop at a traffic light, to go at the traffic light, when to turn, which way to turn, etc.

It was extremely challenging, but God directed us from Batesville to Atlanta safely. I secured the apartment, and God helped us back to Batesville safely despite the same challenges as getting to Atlanta. The following weekend, my mother, stepfather, and sister helped me move permanently to my new apartment in Atlanta. I was elated to start my new journey.

On the other hand, the start of my new journey was much more challenging than I expected. I questioned God about whether it was the right move for me to come to Atlanta. I was alone when my family left to go back to Batesville. I did not know anyone near my area in Georgia. I struggled significantly. I was not 100% independent, including not having my own transportation. It was challenging to go grocery shopping, find a primary care physician, change my social security to Georgia, and to change other information to Georgia without my own transportation.

I did not have much money or food. I had to ration out the food I had. I only had a couple of Hot Pockets, a couple of packs of ramen noodles, bread, eggs, and a frozen pizza. It was depressing. The major times I was away from my apartment were when I used transportation to go to my doctor's appointment at Atlantic Station.

I made mental notes of all the places that I could not afford to visit but would like to visit once I increased my finances. I spent a lot of time praying for guidance, working out, and sitting by the pool at the apartment as I waited to start physical therapy at the Shepherd Center in Atlanta to learn to walk again. However, I did not know I would have to wait longer than six months to start physical therapy.

Although my struggles seemed to last forever, God came through by providing my every need. God reminded me of the scripture He gave me on the way to Atlanta. Joshua 1:9 reads, "Have I not commanded you? Be strong and courageous. Do not be afraid; do not be discouraged, for the Lord your God will be with you wherever you go." God is a God that does not lie.

God kept His promise by placing the right people in my life to help me get everything I needed and wanted. I got a small job as a pool monitor with the help of Sabrina. She also helped me get a MARTA card, cooked for me, and linked me with her friend to go grocery shopping. Mrs. Nessa and her deceased husband, Johnnie, made sure that I ate a home-cooked meal by fixing me a plate every time they cooked. I met friends who were supportive, such as Junior and his wife. My sister, my nephew (Al'Darian; Al), and my niece (Adreanna; Adrea) moved with me as my journey started to look a little brighter.

I was happy my family moved with me. I was not alone anymore. I was happy that my high school friend and football teammate for the South Panola Tigers, Brian Johnson, contacted me after seeing a post on social media stating that I lived in Atlanta. He stated he had been living in Georgia for years and could have been helping me if he'd known I lived in Georgia sooner. He and his wife, Keetra, were significantly helpful. They invited me to their house to eat and helped me with transportation. It was great having a friend from my hometown to hang out with.

I started going to a neurologist at the Shepherd Center. I met a guy in a wheelchair at the Shepherd Center, and he asked me if I was interested in playing wheelchair basketball for the Shepherd Center because I had long arms. I was bored and did not have much going on at home, so I decided to start attending practices to determine if I was interested in playing wheelchair basketball. After observing a few practices, I started participating and joined the basketball team. Wheelchair basketball was much harder to play than it looked. It was very challenging in the beginning. My teammates made wheelchair basketball look easy, including my friend Andrew. As I was starting to like and improve in wheelchair basketball, I was called to start physical therapy.

Although I was having fun with my teammates and new friends, I had a decision to make about continuing wheelchair basketball or putting my all into learning to walk again. I chose to focus on learning to walk again. I quit the basketball team, partially because I did not want to rob the other guys by not being as committed as they were once I got into physical therapy. I put my all into physical therapy. My physical therapist asked me who taught me how to complete tasks in the wheelchair. I told her I taught myself. She placed me in the day program to help me learn effective techniques and ways to complete daily tasks, including transfers, cooking, and bowel training. The therapists observed how helpful I was with helping other wheelchair users use the proper techniques during workouts and encouraging them to finish strong when they were getting tired. I was asked if I was interested in joining the peer support team at the Shepherd Center. I loved helping others, so I automatically said yes.

I gained more benefits by becoming a voluntary peer supporter, including new friends and a job. I was asked if I wanted a job as a surveyor, which paid ten dollars per hour. Although I had a master's degree and wanted better, I accepted the job. I was happy about every blessing, whether small or large, that God gave me. The largest blessing that God gave me during this journey was my ability and strength to stand on the walker with braces and walk. I was proud and grateful to be able to walk down a long hall at the Shepherd Center and for Brian to record a few sessions of me doing so. Two sessions with me walking can be found on YouTube under the titles "Sir Allen's Mission to Walk Part I" and "Part II."

Although physical therapy came to an unexpected halt due to my insurance not paying for it anymore, I was grateful I was almost 100% independent again. The only thing missing was me starting to drive again. The Shepherd Center had a driving program to help wheelchair users get their driver's licenses. I participated in the program and got my first driver's license post-injury in Georgia. I was proud of another accomplishment. However, my car was still in Mississippi. I am grateful for my family, especially my mother, for bringing my car to Georgia from Mississippi.

Now, I was 100% independent and elated that I'd obeyed God by moving to Atlanta. Each area of my life started to get better. I got my first counseling job around 2013. I earned my doctorate degree in Counselor Education and Supervision and Pastoral Counseling in December 2020. I am grateful for Elder Amber K. Abney introducing me to Overseer Steven Shearod because I would not have gone to the Cathedral International Church of Atlanta, Georgia (CICAG) if it was not for her mentioning their church was one of the few churches open during the pandemic when I mentioned to her that God was telling me to go to church. I joined CICAG under the leadership of Overseer Shearod and First Lady Pastor Velicia Shearod.

I became licensed and ordained in Georgia under their leadership, which helped me significantly grow and develop more spiritually. I expanded my private practice, Creating A Difference, LLC, by opening my first office in 2021 with the help of Elder Amber K. Abney. I expanded again after one year by opening a larger suite with the help of family and friends and hiring four therapists by 2023.

Although my journey was challenging due to poor decisions from me and my parents throughout my childhood, my family was very important in shaping me into the man I have become today. My mother, Grandfather L.C., Uncle Harvey and Aunt Linda, and the Pegues family taught me the importance of having a relationship with God. My sister, cousins, and friends helped support me during difficult times. My mother, stepfather, Uncle Harvey, and Aunt Linda played major roles in helping me recover from my spinal cord injury and choose to strive for success by pursuing a higher education and career.

The support from family and friends when I moved to Georgia was needed as I fought through adversity to become successful. Therefore, I hope each person who reads this chapter realizes how important it is to have a supportive family. A supportive family is essential in the growth and development of a person. The choices made by parents throughout a person's childhood can influence if the child grows into a successful man or woman. There is no limit for a person who has a supportive family. A person can accomplish anything he or she puts his or her mind to with the support of family.

Please contact Creating A Difference, LLC if you are in need of mental health or Christian therapy. Most people experience some form of trauma or hurt, whether as a child or as an adult. Do not live in bondage by internalizing your thoughts and feelings. It is good to work through your pain and suffering rather than burying them and not expressing them. Your mental health is just as important as your physical health. Choose to improve your mental health and well-being by contacting a professional to help you work through your concerns. The following is the contact information for Creating A Difference, LLC: 770-906-6473, creatingadifferenceofc@gmail.com, www.creating-a-difference.com, and 4500 Hugh Howell Rd. Ste 230 Tucker, GA 30084.

Chapter 4

Don't Let a Good Life Stop You from Living a Great Life

Baby at the Casino

Every summer as a child, I would go to my maternal grandmother's house in Holly Springs, Mississippi. Man, being there was the highlight of every year for me. We still have one hundred and fifty-four acres to this day.

While other kids were at summer camp, I picked cotton, peas, corn, and beans. I also got to know my mother's side of my family. Man, I loved it. My cousins and I would play basketball and make up other games to play together. I'd cry every time they had to go back to Chicago. Marico and Marvell came to Grandma's each year with fancy clothes and fancy Jordans. They called me a city boy even though my upbringing was country as hell. Rico was a prolific basketball player; I grew up wanting to be *just* like him.

My best childhood memory was with my favorite cousin, Buster, at twelve years old. He would visit Grandma's every other summer. Buster took me to the store and told me to get whatever I wanted. I got three boxes of chocolate candy. Man, I was amazed! I went home and told my mom, "I want to be like cousin Buster!" Oh, boy. Mom tried to keep me away from Buster. Buster was her nephew, but as she was the baby of all her siblings, he was her age.

A drug dealer from Chicago who had a *lot* of authority, Buster is 30 years older than me. He had fur coats, Cadillacs, and a wallet full of money—*and* he was ordering grown men around! *Sheesh!* When I first saw him in action—coming to Mississippi from Chicago, seven cars deep, with men who worked for him—I immediately thought, *That's what I want.* I became infatuated with Buster; I wanted to know everything about him. How could I not?

My dad, Charles Edward Prater, was from Natchez, Mississippi, which is *completely* different from Holly Springs. It's more urban than rural, with more modern things, but it's still considered the country. My paternal grandparents had a nice house, and my granddad drove a Cadillac. We'd visit them for Christmas, and *everything*—food, desserts, I mean *everything*—was in abundance. My granddad gave me my first car, a 1984 Seville. He was old school and loved deer hunting. My dad followed his dad's footsteps, but I just couldn't get into it. I never wanted to be hunting out in the cold.

My dad was extremely hardworking. He came home every day from work and maintained a full-fledged farm., pulled out mail, and went through it, muttering, "Always looking at these damn bills." He was stressed due to bills and dealing with white people, and I just knew from observing him that I never wanted to work a job. I admired my dad for his commitment to our family and being a provider. I would see him sometimes frustrated with the bills and that inspired me to want to be a successful entrepreneur. We didn't see eye to eye.

My mom, Mary Lou Bean, was the baby of twelve children in a family of sharecroppers who worked on a plantation. She was an office worker at Bar Elementary School. She made a lot of money. I'm a proud Mama's boy. I love her to death; there isn't anything she didn't or wouldn't do for us as a mother. She was impressively savvy with finances. When we went Christmas shopping or school shopping, we would always have to buy clothes with the red tag for an extra 30% off; we never bought anything at full price, and we always ordered from the 99-cent menu.

I was raised in a two-parent home, and I always had a comfortable roof over my head. Outside of the home, though, comfort was not so abundant. Due to peak gang activity, we moved from the inner city to the country in 1992 when I was ten or eleven years old. Dad found a thirty-acre farm for us, and we lived the farm life—lots of trees, ghost chickens, cows, goats, gardening, gathering wood for the fireplace, driving into the city to go to school or run errands, all of it. After school, I'd come home and pick pecans from our twenty-eight pecan trees; picking pecans and selling them at school was one of my side hustles. I'd help my mom around the house, and my daddy would come home from work and make sure everything was together. Living the country life was depressing for me at times. I went to a country school for ninth and tenth grade, and I was always failing. I couldn't find my way there. I was always a city boy at heart.

I'll just say it: Mississippi is a racist state, no matter where you go. I always wanted to leave and experience life elsewhere; I couldn't stay in Mississippi my entire life. Once, we spent all day picking butter beans, then went to the store to sell them. I gave the worker—a white man—the bushels, and he threw the change over the counter at us. I threw that change right back at the man. My mild-mannered cousins told me not to, but I wasn't tolerating the disrespect.

My parents met at Jackson State University. My father only went for a year or two, pledged, and joined the Navy. The next thing you knew, he was in Italy in 1972. Then, he came back and married my mom. I'm the middle child of three boys, and I'm different from my two brothers. They are the "model brothers"; one is four years younger than me, and the other is two years older than me. I was always the son who got whoopings. I was a little outgoing, and my grades were a bit below average.

My brothers love my children dearly.and treat me fine. Recently, I had a phone call with my older brother, Jamal, and I told him that I love him and I need him around. He's one hell of a big brother, and it took me forty-two years here on earth to break it down and truly realize that. My younger brother Mensah, spoils the hell out of them too. He lives in Los Angeles, California. We had the time of our lives when we visited Universal Studios. We made some special memories on that trip! Everybody spoils my kids; at the end of the day, it's all about how the kids are doing. Now, I try to be the best brother I can and take advantage because I was pretty harsh toward my brothers growing up. I love them, and I appreciate them. I wouldn't be anything without my brothers, and family's all we've got. Family will always be there to support you when no one else is, and they can be gone in an instant. Never wait until it's too late to tell your loved ones that you love them.

Dead Presidents

Do you remember the first time you tasted one of your favorite foods? I do. One of my favorite foods is tacos. There was this Mexican restaurant in Mississippi called El Chico. I'm not lying to you when I tell you that their chicken tacos are a ten out of ten. They taste like what I imagine food tastes like in heaven—angelic. I remember the first time experiencing the burst of flavors and how it was love at first bite.

That was my exact level of excitement when I held my first paycheck in my hand. I was sixteen years old when I started working at Krystal. I hated damn near everything about working at Krystal. People are something else when they are hungry, but the dealbreaker for me was smelling like onions. I would leave the restaurant and smell like a bag of chopped onions until I took a shower. I was disgusted by that aroma and ended up quitting.

After getting my own check and having the freedom to do my own thing with my money, I had to find another way to make money. I was not going to let the smell of onions stand in my way of getting paper, so I interviewed at FootAction and started working there. This was a much better environment for me. I liked the culture and I liked shoes, and that was good enough for me. Plus, unlike Krystal—or any other fast-food restaurant for that matter—I MADE A COMMISSION. And that became my only mission. I was also attending Raymond High School at the time, and there, I excelled. I played football and began to grow into my personality.

Selling the most expensive shoes to maximize my paycheck was my game plan. It may not seem like a lot now, but eight to nine dollars for each pair of Jordans equaled out to sometimes making $150 in commission alone on my checks. This sparked my excitement surrounding money, and it opened my mind to possibilities of what making money could do for me.

Not only that, but having my own money boosted my self-confidence. Man, not having to ask my parents for stuff that I wanted was a game changer. Back when I was at FootAction, I remember showing my dad my paycheck. The smile on his face expressed to me that he was both impressed and proud—"That's what I'm talking about!" He took the check out of my hand and took a closer look at it before pulling me into his warm embrace. "Every man needs to make his own money; that's how he finds his way."

Looking back, I appreciate making money and experiencing all the benefits that come along with it. I was young and blew through most of my money. I was irresponsible; I was a young man without any real responsibilities or bills, so my money ended up in malls, restaurants, and right back to the place that I got my check in the first place: FootAction.

I might have fallen too deeply in love with money, to be honest. I was so focused on my money that I lost sight of my schoolwork. I would go to school, but if I was given the choice to go get some money or go to school, man, I chose the money. My grades started to reflect my low interest in schoolwork.

It was my senior year at Jim Hill High School. It was progress report time, and my grades were not where they needed to be for me to graduate on time. No amount of money in the world would save me from my parents or the jokes of my brothers and friends if I didn't tighten up and graduate from high school. I was forced to find a balance of both getting to the money and making the grade. I attended summer school and received my diploma. I didn't get to walk with my class across the stage, but I graduated that summer! That was important to me because I was ready to show my parents that I could be responsible, and I wanted to leave Mississippi immediately. I had my eyes set on relocating to Atlanta, Georgia. I would always hear from my aunt and uncle how exciting things were in Atlanta. I knew that the big city would be my next home.

Welcome to Atlanta, Where the Players Play

As it relates to money, looking back, this phase of my life prepared me for what was to come down the road. A few years later, my financial life changed dramatically out of nowhere, and it all started at Clark Atlanta University in Atlanta, Georgia ... where the players play. Going to college opened my eyes and gave me opportunities to provide for myself and my family in ways that I never imagined possible.

When I stepped on the Promenade of Clark Atlanta University (CAU) to visit my cousin who was already enrolled there, it was as though I stepped into a video shoot for Lil John or Lil John and the Eastside Boys mixed with Outkast. The energy was transformative. There was fashion, music, and beautiful Black people. Everybody had their own vibe that they brought from their hometown, an array of styles. At one point, I had to stop and lean on one of the large, brick flower pot dividers that lined the center of the campus walkway called the Promenade.

I saw the fellows with dreadlocks, low fades, baggy pants, white tees, some business students with three-piece suits on, and even the Greek letters that I saw my dad rock: Omega Psi Phi. Then, there were the ladies. *Lord, have mercy!* I couldn't tell you what they had on, but what I can remember is their beautiful skin colors, beautiful smiles, and bodacious bodies. And on top of that, they were carrying books. Brown bodies and brains—I knew this was the place where I needed to be, especially considering that I was attending a school that was the complete opposite. *How in the hell did I end up at Concordia College in Selma, Alabama?* was my first thought.

The answer to that question was simple. Concordia was one of the first places that I got accepted to, and it wasn't far from home. Being there took me back in time; everything and everywhere was outdated, stuck in the past, and slow-paced. It's a Christian school, so there were rules on top of rules. Strict was an understatement. Although it wasn't the ideal college experience that I was looking for, it provided me more freedom than being home.

I am grateful for the encounters and exposure I experienced at Concordia. I found myself experiencing major life events later in life. I took my first sip of alcohol, had sex for the first time, and even smoked weed in college. All of this was mainly because of my country lifestyle. I really didn't have access to things. We lived on a farm, and outside of school, we didn't do a whole lot. In fact, we lived about thirty minutes away from town.

I met my lifelong friend, Red, from Birmingham there. We only spent one year of college together, our freshman year, and that's all it took for me to recognize that he would be like a brother to me for the rest of our lives. You ever heard the saying, "Some family members disguise themselves as friends"? Well, that was the case with Red—a friendship that still exists to this day.

We met moving into the dorm. Red's parents and older younger sister were helping move him in. For some reason, I thought that his sister was attending the school, too. She was very pretty. and I started making plans for our immediate future. Imagine my disappointment when I found out that one of the few Black girls there was not a student at Concordia.

Everything works out as it should because that very next year, I left Concordia and enrolled into CAU after witnessing Black excellence that life-changing day on the Promenade. Seeing how everyone was making their moves made me want to figure out how to get my money right. So, after transferring to CAU, I got a job at Rich's department store, which is now Macy's.

We Gettin' Money Over Here

One thing I know for sure is that Atlanta was—and still is—a home for schemers and dreamers. If you can dream it up, you can find a scam to finance it. After working there for several months, a couple of guys who also worked there showed me what they were doing to make thousands of dollars on the side. They would take their Rich's card and let people buy whatever they wanted in the store, then load the funds back onto their Rich's card as if the items were never purchased. They would also sell clothes, stolen merchandise.

Access to FUBU, Polo, and all the other hottest brands, plus the students at CAU, equaled *mo' money, mo' money, mo'!* Then, I got another easy job as a freelance model. This was my best job. For twenty dollars an hour, I handed out samples of perfume and submitted my timesheet to my boss, who was in New York City. I would say that I worked for forty hours every week; meanwhile, I was at home or Rich's. Then, on one of my days off, a coworker told me that loss prevention was looking for me. The gig was up. I didn't return to that store for years, not even as a customer.

I was working and scheming because I did not have financial aid. I had to sit a semester out because I missed the deadline to apply for financial aid, although my transfer was successful. I ended up moving into Brawley Hall. I met the campus weed man in the rec. room. We kicked it off playing pool and ended up being roommates.

During this time, I felt like I had the weight of the world on my shoulders. I was depressed about not being in school, having loss prevention on my mind, and pledging. I was pre-pledging and had been for quite some time. The guys were playing games with when our line was going to cross, and I felt like they couldn't break me mentally, since I was already dealing with a lot. They ended up saying that they were not having that line.

I was fed up and needed to do something fun. I told my roommate, "Man, I'm done with this shit. Let's throw a party." We threw a party at a house off of Hamilton E. Holmes Drive. We gave out free weed and alcohol. It was jam-packed. The following week, we threw another party, and it was just as packed. Three of my friends and I formed New South Entertainment as party promoters.

This was in 2003 at the height of Black Mob Family (BMF). Atlanta was on fire. We had outgrown the houses, and we needed more space, so we began renting out clubs in Buckhead. We were at Club Fluid and Club Chaos. Three weeks later, we were cashing out with $20,000 to split four ways for our weekend parties. I became a party promoter by default.

The following year, my fraternity of choice had officially announced that they were having a line. By this time, my interest had changed. I had changed. It was etched in my mind that fraternity life was no longer for me. We kept throwing parties, and then I graduated in 2005.

You're All I Need to Get By

I met my girlfriend, Amira, who is now my wife, at a party at Club 1150. She attended Spelman. What stood out to me about her, other than her obvious beauty, was that she was not like the other young women I met in my line of work. She wasn't easily impressed by my money or my status. We would party together and grab food afterwards. She didn't eat meat. She cared about her health. She also drove a nice car and stayed in nice apartments. My money was not going to influence her. All of those things made her different in the best way. She was the first—and only—woman I made my girlfriend. My wife has been a constant reminder of love, patience, and kindness. She has had so much faith in me that I have been able to borrow from her. When someone loves you unconditionally, you can't help but do your best and show up as your best self. It's been twenty years, and three kids later, we are still rocking. Our beautiful family keeps me going! I love you, Caniah, Charles, and Theo! They are my "why."

During the tough times, she was solid. We both graduated in 2005, and we moved in together. I did not know what I wanted to do with my life as far as my career goals. I picked up odd jobs here and there. A year after I graduated from CAU, my cousin introduced me to a friend of his who wanted to buy some weed, and the man who had the weed was the Atlanta University Center (AUC) library man, KB! He had nice clothes, all the designer clothes, shit—he could afford all of the nice things that we wanted in dated all the girls we liked in college. He showed me the game and ended up becoming my mentor later in life. I wanted to be just like KB. He had a family, an Escalade truck, and lived in a beautiful home.

Money Ain't a Thang

The guy who wanted the weed bought three pounds' worth at first. Then, the next time he returned, he bought five pounds. The guy from the library gave me $300 for the transaction. Then, he gave $500 for the next one. Guy wanted to come back from Mississippi and get some more weed—it went from three pounds to 100 pounds! I was fresh out of college, and I went from having no money to getting $10,000 every ten days. I didn't know that I was getting into the game as a "broker." Within months, I was picking up $15,000 to $20,000 every two weeks, and all I had to do to get my cut was take this man to the library. We had shoeboxes full of money. We shopped at designer stores and ate at the best restaurants, ordering everything on the menu.

My future wife went back to school, got her master's degree, and entered an exchange program in China. We traveled internationally. We just did it big. All of this was because I was a street broker. My name started to spread, and when people from Mississippi visited, I could get them what they wanted—girls, drugs, and entry to the dopest parties. I offered a VIP experience to the ATL city life. This went on from 2006 to 2008.

Mo' Money, Mo' Problems

When visiting Amira in China in 2006, I started an import export business buying counterfeit luxury handbags and shoes. I would buy a high-end shoe for thirty-five dollars and sell it for $350. After one of my trips to China, I got robbed. On the wrong side of town one night, I opened my trunk to sell some of the goods (clothes, weed, bags). Some guys pulled a gun on me and took everything, including my car. *Damn.* I got caught slipping in my car, which was full of my latest shipment. I realized that I was being greedy and stupid. I was moving my products like I was selling candy bars. I learned my lesson from that incident and tightened up.

Then, there were issues with my business partners. Most of them ended up in prison, but I was saved by my decisions not to participate in the things that they were participating in. Some of them were jealous because I didn't go to prison. I would talk to them, and they would reference how they were in prison while I was out here with my family.

Made a Way

In the spring of 2011, I was really down on my luck. I'd hit rock bottom. My wife was pregnant with our first child, and I didn't have money for food. I decided to go into the cafeteria at Clark to sneak food. At that time, I ran into Constance Booth, a fashion coordinator from CAU. She invited me to a meeting that was previously introduced to me by Elliot Tabron introduced me to the concept of network marketing. I tried that out for a while, but like most of my get-rich-quick schemes, it eventually dried up, too. I learned personal development and my life began to change for the better.

When I say I hit rock bottom, I mean *rock bottom*. I started going to Vegas, and ... well, I just started gambling. Blackjack is my game of choice. Gambling can bring out really bad emotions and turn a person into a bad one. I got used to spending money; I'd gone from window shopping to becoming a preferred vendor at Louis Vuitton. I became obsessed with not being able to afford luxuries.

Oftentimes, I couldn't pay bills, but when it's good, man, it's great! When I'm balling like that, I can go buy my wife anything she wants. I like to splurge. We go to nice restaurants and order everything on the menu. In fact, I had my first steak as an adult! I've gone to Dubai with first-class trips on the Emirates airline, taken exotic trips to St. Barts, Lake Como, Monaco, Greece—anything you see in *Forbes*, I've done it.

My addiction got so bad that we'd go to Vegas, I'd tell my wife I'd be right back, and she wouldn't see me for another day and a half. I'd come back to the room drunk, and it'd make any wife mad. I mean, I was coming back drunk, having lost all my money and messed up the savings. I once lost $60,000 playing blackjack.

My wife always knew I lost money by what I told her—how much I love her, how much I appreciate her. "You don't tell me all this unless you lost a lot of money," she would say. "I can't keep doing this. You need to go to therapy." She threatened to leave. I would tell her I'd get help, but never did. I'd simply sell drugs to get the money back. The stress of not having money led to resentment from my wife. She'd be emotionally disconnected, not wanting to be touched.

I started taking drugs in 2022. I was feeling depressed after the COVID-19 outbreak, and a friend gave me a Perc (Percocet). It made me so relaxed. I soon realized that I couldn't function without the pills. I started self-regulating and went from popping one to sometimes three pills each day. I still struggle with this addiction, but I've already made great strides toward sobriety.

My advice? Stay away from gambling and drugs; don't do them at all. Nothing is more important than your loved ones, than family. Drugs and money will distract you from that. Money comes and goes, and friends come and go, but family is forever. I've had money and I've had nothing. The thing about fast money is that it goes just as fast as it comes. A good friend told me, "Don't let a good life stop you from living a great life." To me, that means there is always room for improvement and bettering your circumstances, even if you're comfortable with the way things are.

I'm proud to say that I am now fully legit. I'm a go-getter! I'm always going to hustle; it's in my DNA, and I've learned a lot about being a businessman. I am a real estate investor, I am opening a restaurant this year, and I invest in the cannabis industry. To get to where I am now, I had to change three things: the things I listened to, the books I read, and the people whom I hung around. I started feeding my mind and my spirit more positivity with uplifting music, thought-provoking literature, and my circle of go-getter friends, and man, it works!

It's not an easy adjustment. This was where my faith was activated. Habits are hard as hell to change, and fighting addictions makes things even more difficult. I can't do this alone; I am inspired by my family to be the best man I can be. I've changed my mindset from limitations to abundance.

I am anchored by my faith to leave behind my *good* life and continue to strive to live my *great* life.

Charles Prater

Chapter 5

STANDING TALL BY THE GRACE OF GOD

"Man that is born of a woman is of a few days and full of trouble."
— Job 14:1

No one or no family should have to deal with family tragedy—at the very least, not a nine-year-old trying to figure out why there is so much dismay and discord going around in the family. But there I was, a nine-year-old trying to process why I could not see my big sister that day or forever more.

We came from a small town called Dunnellon, Florida, which is in the central Florida area. On this particular day, the entire family was in a panic because for twenty-four hours, there had been no sign of my older sister, Beverly Shawn Jefferies, and my first cousin, Aundry Bostick. No one had any idea as to their whereabouts. In this small town, it was pretty much a classic as to what you would hear about small towns: Everyone knew each other, and all of the older folks knew all of the kids to our parents.

By many standards, we would have been considered poor, but we didn't know it because we always seemed to get everything we wanted. It was a tight-knit community, and everyone looked out for each other, especially looking out for the kids. On this particular day, everyone was frantic as family members and law enforcement were in a search of my sister and my cousin. As the day came to a close, we started getting news of my missing sister and cousin. As night fell, we all got the word that my sister and my cousin were dead.

They had both drowned together in the city's only lake earlier that day. We were devastated. I could not believe it. I had lost my big sister, the girl who protected her little brother. Yes, I said protect her little brother, but isn't it supposed to be the other way around, that I should be protecting my sister? But there it is: My big sister was gone at ten years old and a close cousin at nine years. My family and I suffered a hurt that hit deep within our souls, and there was no way to process our feelings during those days. So, I did what every kid would do: I sat around and cried most of the time. I was always told I was a bit of a crybaby and a Mommy's boy growing up, but those traits would mold me into the type of man that I came to be.

As we were proceeding with the funeral, I still can see the two caskets sitting there with my sister and cousin, just thinking, *They will get up any time now.* This had to be some crazy mix-up joke that involved my sister; it was just not happening. But that was not the case. We buried them, and for a long time, there was a big hole in my heart as I knew that I would never see my big sister or cousin, my protector and my friend. But as they say, all things get better with time.

As the years went by, we slowly began to heal. Seeing my mother come through the ordeal left a few scars; she would never trust any of her kids around water again. That posed a problem for me. Because of the deaths of my sister and cousin, I didn't want anyone else in the family to die due to drowning, so I did what any other kid would do: I snuck off to swimming lessons without letting my mother know until I was well into the lessons. After the lessons were over, I encouraged my mother to come to the city beach to watch me swim. I was hoping to ease her mind, knowing that one of her kids had learned to swim.

She did come out to see me, but for the first hour or so, she would not even look at me to know if I could swim or not. She eventually did, and her mind was put somewhat at ease. That action did open the door for my other sisters and brothers to try and learn to swim. Not all were successful; my baby sister was having no parts of it, and my younger brothers did try. Terry and Kenneth (a.k.a. Porky) did learn, but my brother Stephen did not. He just decided to just stay away from the water. I spent the rest of the time growing up in the role of the eldest, with everyone looking up to me for direction and my mother depending on me more and more.

As I went through my middle school and high school years, there would be more drama to come for our household. In my eleventh-grade year, my mother and father decided to separate and divorce. That made me the unquestioned man of the house. So, taking care of my sister and brothers and working became part of the norm while, at the same time, I tried to decide on a career path once I left high school. I did have ambitions, too.

I didn't want to be one of those guys I saw hanging around town under trees drinking, smoking dope, and just wasting away each and every day. But what was my mother going to do? Who was to help her? Who in the house was going to step up and help earn some money to assist her if I left? I didn't know what I was going to do; I just knew I couldn't stay there and waste away.

As I made my way through school, I became a pretty good basketball player. I also was a decent football player "despite my size"—I was only 150 pounds soaking wet. I was also a track star and a cross country athlete, so I managed to keep busy along with helping to take care of the home and getting good grades. The extracurricular activity that would get me into college was music. I was also in the marching band and very talented, if I must say so myself. That would all be for nothing if I could not go, and staying home to help the family was the top priority at the time. The deciding voice came from the only person who could give it to me: my mother. My mother told me the story of her going through school. You see, when she was in high school, she was an outstanding basketball player, and she was offered a scholarship to attend Bethune-Cookman College (now University) to play basketball. She could not attend because she became pregnant with me. So, I had the opportunity to go where she gave up and become among the first generation of college students in the family.

I decided to attend Bethune Cookman College after receiving a music scholarship in the fall of 1979. I was so happy to be attending, and things would never be the same again. The race was on for a chance for me to make a difference and to maybe ease some of the pressure as the eldest adult in the house.

The race is not given to the swift or the fast but to the one who endureth to the end. — Ecclesiastes 9:11

I knew college life for me would be a game changer. After all, I was going to a school that had a ratio of eight to one girls to guys, and I was going to be a part of the most famous group on the entire campus, the Marching Wildcats. As a young eighteen-year-old, I walked onto the campus with my chest out. No one could tell me anything.

Like any other freshman, I didn't know what to think when I walked onto campus. Being in the band, we had to report to campus two weeks before the rest of the student body; just us, the band and the football team.

At that time, there was no one to see you other than those you are working with and the staff. We practiced three times a day: one session in the band room studying music, and the other two on the field in the hot sun running, conditioning, and learning new formations. Coming from high school, this was something totally different for me. We did not practice like this; it was not this hard. We were dirtier than the football team every day, and we ate lunch last and by ourselves.

The first week, I thought it sucked, and I wanted to go home. But I knew if I did that, my mother would be very disappointed; after all, in the small town of Dunnellon, she had told everyone about her son who was in the band at Bethune-Cookman, so running home was not an option. I didn't want anyone to think I was weak and couldn't hang, so I buckled down and took care of business.

Those two weeks passed, and then the rest of the student body began to arrive on the campus. I, like everyone else, hung around the freshmen women's dorm because that was where all of the new ladies would be. I don't know why that was a big deal for me because I was new on the campus myself. All the other guys were there, so I went there, as well. I slowly settled into college life—classes, making new friends, looking at fraternities, and just getting a routine down, trying to balance rigorous band practice with classes and everything else I wanted to experience.

The one thing that quickly became apparent was that the band had followers—some might even say we also had groupies. The fans and groupies would be at band practice every day, watching us, yelling and cheering for us from the sidelines. If we did certain dance moves in practice, they would get even louder. That's how it was when I met that girl—the girl who would eventually change my life in more ways than I thought possible.

Malinda Rachelle Pandy was that girl; she would come to see me practice every day and would catcall me from the sideline if we did a dance that was a little provocative. She did not go to any other area of the practice field. She stayed directly in front of me every day, yelling at me from the sideline.

Then, one day, she decided to get a little bolder and approach me. She called me over to the sideline one day after practice and wanted to talk. She got right to the point; she introduced herself to me, we exchanged some pleasantries, and she then said to me, "Would you like to come over to my house for dinner?" I, of course, accepted, and I made plans to meet her there. Chelle was a very beautiful girl with a great figure and a wonderful personality, but you know how most guys at eighteen or nineteen think—hey, it was a way to get in the house.

My mother, Shirly, taught me to be respectful of everyone, but hormones start to kick in, and they take you in a different direction. I will say, though, that nothing happened that time, and I was very respectful to her. When we first met, I didn't even like her. I thought she was very nice but not my type. I got to give it to her—she was very persistent when she saw something she liked or someone she wanted to be around, so she did not give up or give in. She stayed the course. She slowly began to win me over, and we became closer and closer.

It eventually got to a point where we thought it was time to meet her family. So, we set up a time to meet her parents and her sisters and brothers. Now, you know whether you feel welcomed by someone by the way they speak to you. Her family looked me over, and they seemed to be a little standoffish. I chalked it up as the first time meeting, with us not really knowing each other. She had three brothers and four sisters, with one of the sisters being her twin.

As time went on, the brothers never seemed to warm up to me, and I felt like they just didn't like me at all. I didn't care because I didn't think much of them, either, so there was always friction between us. As far as the sisters are concerned, they were a little softer. They always seemed to show some apprehension about me, but I was always able to communicate with them. Chelle's second oldest sister is who I was able to communicate with the most.

As far as the parents, I guess I got mixed emotions. The father was pretty quiet, and the mother was the more vocal person of the two. I just got the feeling she did not trust me with her daughter, which is understandable; she is a mother thinking about her child's well-being.

Chelle and I dated the rest of my college career, and in my senior year at Cookman, Chelle was pregnant with our child. I finished my senior year, and I graduated in 1983 with a degree in business administration. I had five job offers, and I chose to work for the Walgreens in management, so I was on to the next phase of my career. The plan was to go down to Tampa, get myself established, and have Chelle move down. I started with the company on June 13, 1983, which was the same day my first son was born.

Tampa was the place I'd always wanted to live in. My cousin was there, and he often told me that he wanted me to come down there when I graduated from college. I did. The move and job were not easy at the time because I lived in Tampa but worked in Sarasota, where my Walgreens store was located. I had to travel fifty-five miles one way every day, so that was a one-hundred-and-ten-mile trip every day with an unreliable car. I can't tell you how many times I broke down beside the road and how many times my cousin had to come pick me up. This went on for about three months before they actually transferred me into the city of Tampa. I eventually settled into the store and my own place. The thought of Chelle not being here constantly pushed me to get the things in place that I needed so that she and my son could get here and we could start a life for ourselves.

The job began to come out fine; I was excelling in every area of the job, and I was being recognized for the work that I was doing. After about eight or nine months, I was ready to bring Chelle and my son down to Tampa. I made the trip back to Daytona Beach to get them. She, of course, was ready to go, and I was ready to get them. Her family was not as sure they wanted to see her go, so there were constant reminders from her parents to take care of their daughter and from her siblings to take care of their sister.

I eventually got Chelle and my son moved down to Tampa. I had found a little two-bedroom place on the east side of town. It wasn't very much, but it was ours, and most importantly, we were together. That was all I cared about. We were doing well as a family; I worked, and she stayed home to take care of the house and our son. Things were going really well, and a few months later, Chelle became pregnant with another child on the way.

This time, things were different; we did not really find out until late in the pregnancy, so there was not prenatal care until late, but the most serious issue was she was having heart problems brought on by my firstborn, which were made more serious by the pregnancy of our second child. It was discovered that Chelle had developed a heart murmur, or a small hole in her heart, that was worsened by the birth of our children. So, after close to a year, I had to do something I did not want to do: take her back to Daytona, to her home, so that there would be family to watch over her.

I was truly hurt that she had to go back, that this kind of life-threatening issue had come up, and that I played a part in her health issues. I felt guilty because I got her pregnant. I should have asked more questions or deeper questions about our health and well-being. Once I got her back to Daytona, she was admitted to the hospital for care and to be watched.

For the next couple of months, when I was off, I made the trip to Daytona as often as I could; it still seemed like it was never enough. I also felt like there were some people in the family who thought I should have been there more, as well. I still had to work and earn a living, so I tried to make sure I spent my time in both areas when I could. I was getting constant feedback from her sister on her condition. Our daughter was born in January, and shortly after that, there was a steady decline in Chelle's health condition.

I was not in Daytona when our daughter was born. I wanted to be there, but I stayed and worked until I was free. On a day not much later, I received a call from her sister letting me know that Chelle had coded: "Her heart stopped." I was then told that she was revived and alert. I immediately requested time off, and I went to Daytona to visit her. When I got there, I was so glad to see her, and all I could think about was her coming back to Tampa with me. I know I was being selfish, but I still wanted her with me. After all, she was the girl I was going to marry.

By then, my relationship with most of the family had become very rocky, at the least. I don't know why or how it got that way, but it was, and I thought they held me accountable for Chelle's health condition. Maybe they were right; maybe I was to blame. However you look at it, I felt bad. While I visited with Chelle, we talked at length. I let her know how much I missed her, how much I cared, and how much I wanted to have her back with me in Tampa. Chelle expressed to me how much she cared for me, so much so that she gave me two children.

I then got the sense that she knew what her health condition was, and telling me that only reinforced how much she cared for me, knowing that there would or could be complications. After I left and returned back to Tampa, little did I know that this trip would be the last time I would hear her voice or see her alive. With a newborn baby not even a month old, I got the call from her sister telling me Chelle had died.

I was at work when I got the call. The only thing that I can remember was immediately breaking down in the office of the store, with my store manager frantically asking me what was going on and what was happening. I stayed on the phone with her sister for a while, and she was constantly asking me if I was okay. I really believe she was concerned for me, and I truly think she was the one person who really knew how I felt about Chelle.

As we got closer to the funeral, there was some drama brewing that I could not understand. There seems to be a plot brewing by one or two of the brothers and another member of the family to jump me and beat me up on the day of the funeral.

I don't remember how I got the information about the supposed fight, but my cousin was still living in Daytona still. He knew a few people, and some of those in that family didn't realize he was related to me. When I got the information, I did what any other Black male who had a chip on their shoulder would do. I went home and got my boys to come to the funeral with me. I am not proud of this because we were supposedly there to celebrate the life of someone who was very dear to me and I loved, but I did. As the funeral went on at the church, there were no problems, but once we got to the graveside and the final words were said, there were two people making a beeline straight at me. The only thing I could think was, *It's on.*

As they approached me, one began to get loud, and the people I brought turned and were ready to respond for me. Those guys were my cousins, and some of them lived to fight, so they were there ready for a get-down. I was still feeling pretty bad as this was about to go down, but God was on time. There were several people who saw what was about to happen, intervened, and stopped anyone from making a mockery of her home. But from that point on, the decisions that I made after the funeral impacted me and my children to this very day.

In the days after the funeral, I decided to allow my daughter to remain with her grandparents. I took my son with me to Tampa for a short while, then brought him back to Daytona for his grandparents to keep him. I don't know why I didn't go back to get both of them. I had a lot of things running through my head—how I could take care of them, my career—and to some degree, I was just scared and didn't know what to do. It was a decision I really regretted, but I did what I thought was best for all of us.

"You don't get in life what you want; you get in life what you are."

"But by the grace of God I am what I am." — 1 Corinthians 15:10"

I soon settled into a routine in Tampa, with work taking up the bulk of my time. I focused a lot of time on my career; I wanted to get promoted as fast as I could. I then got out into the social scene a bit. Hey, if I work hard, I party just as hard. I dated from time to time, but I did not want to get into any serious relationships. I guess, as they say, I became somewhat of a player, but I figured, *Why not?* Two years into my post-college time, I had lost the one most important person to me. But not long after, I met a girl that I worked with, and she and I started to date. We dated for seven years, which is a long time not to have taken it further. We did make an attempt, but needless to say, it didn't work, and we decided to go our separate ways.

In the spring of 1992, I had to leave and go home again because there was another loss in the family. My mom's oldest sister had died of cancer. I was very close to all of my aunts, and as a family, we took it very hard. Going home to deal with the loss of my aunt, I was expected, as always, to be the rock and strength of our house. Maybe these are the expectations I set on myself; being the eldest, in most crises, the family looks to me for leadership and a calming voice. We buried our aunt, and I returned to my life back in Tampa.

As time went by, I did have the longing for a more serious relationship, but it seemed to not happen while I was looking. But you know the old saying: It will usually hit you when you least expect it. On one Saturday in October, one of the Divine Nine sororities was having a Halloween costume party, and a couple of brothers and I decided to go. When my brothers and I got there, you can understand that there were a ton of ladies at the party.

Let's say they were the organization that wore red, if you know what I mean. So, as my brothers and I looked around to size up the crowd, I looked across the room. There, I saw the girl sitting at the table with friends, just chillin' and checking out the surroundings. I said to my brothers, "There are some girls at that table. Let's go over and ask if they want to dance." I figured I had some inroads because I knew two of the ladies from college.

Well, my brothers didn't want to come with me, so I went by myself and struck up a conversation with the two that I knew. I asked the one to dance, the one who belongs to the sorority. When she got up to go dance with me, she had on a tight red devil costume, and as I followed her to the dance floor, I was thinking,

Damnnn!!! to myself. I was like *Man, she's fine. This is the one right here. I am not going home without getting her number and finding out if I can see her again.*

As the song ended, she decided she was going to leave, and I did what any other brother would do: I walked her to her car and gave her my number. I didn't get hers; maybe she thought I was a crazy person and didn't trust me. So, I didn't know if she was interested or not. But to my surprise, a couple of days later, guess who showed up at my job! The girl in the red devil outfit. I was very happy to see her, and on that visit, she asked me if I would like to go on an outing with her. I did accept, and the girl in the red devil outfit later became my wife.

Cannella and I got married April 16, 1995, Easter Sunday. Soon after, we decided that we wanted to have a change of scenery to start our marriage, so we decided to move to Tallahassee, Florida to raise the girls and to start our family life fresh. Everything was in place as far as our careers and all the things that came with it. When we got to Tallahassee, we quickly decided that we would like a house instead of renting and doing the apartment thing long-term.

We followed the plan, and after a few months, we started construction on our new house. It took maybe six to seven months before the house was completed, and when it was, we moved in and finally settled into our new city and home. We moved into our house in February, and sometime during the summer, my dad came to visit me.

Again, he was my stepdad, but that didn't really matter to me; he was the only person I knew in my toddler years. I was so happy for him to come. I wanted him to meet my new family and see the home that we built, and I wanted to just enjoy some time with him. I could have never guessed that it would be the last time that I would see my father. The following October, I got a call telling me that the man who had taught me baseball, supported me in track and field, and was behind me when I decided to use band as a catalyst to college had died.

I was, again, devastated. Another trip to my home of Dunnellon to bury someone else I cared about. We buried our father toward the end of October, and again, I was in a period of mourning. I would soon learn there would be more to come. In the next month, November, my family was out of town visiting family in Tampa, and I spent the day relaxing, watching football.

The one thing about retail was you didn't get to travel much with family because you would usually be required to work the next day. As for me, after that holiday, the next day was called Black Friday in the retail world. I went to work, got to my job site, and sat in the parking lot for a few minutes before I decided to go into the store. Before I could get out of the car, I received a call from my mother telling me that my brother Steve, the one right under me, had just died on Thanksgiving night. I sat in the car, shocked. I immediately broke down in the car and cried for the next five to ten minutes.

She needed me to come home ASAP because she just felt lost and didn't know what to do. I don't even remember calling someone from work to come in to replace me; I just started the engine of my car and headed home to pack. All I could think was, *I just buried my father, and a month later, I'm burying my brother.* As I prepared to go home, I packed as fast as I could and set out on the trip home to assist and to make sure my mother was okay. I was still shocked and a little frantic as I set out on the road home.

On my way home, I was still crying so much while I was driving that I almost got in an accident. I almost ran off the road into a wooded area. I had to stop in the next city and sit in the car for a few minutes and gather myself before I could continue home. I knew that hurting myself would not be good for anyone, so I sat for a few minutes, ate something, and then continued my journey home. The worst thing about getting the news about my brother was the fact that the last time he and I did speak, we had somewhat of an argument.

Brothers argue, it was what all families did, but the problem with this was our insults were the last things that he and I said to each other the last time we saw each other. That would haunt me for a long time. I would not get a chance to tell him sorry or how much I loved him, or to just give him a big hug and let him know everything is all good. No more second chances; my brother was gone. My mother always tried to look strong, but I knew she was hurting and doing her best to hold it together in front of us. After we buried my father and brother, we went through the rest of the year as best we could, but the following year took a different turn.

> *"They are brought to their knees and fall,*
> *but we rise up and stand firm."* — Psalms 20:8

I have learned over the years to follow scripture that says, "Cast no cares for tomorrow; live for today, and let tomorrow's concerns take care of themselves." It soon became a realization to me that the only time it seemed our family would get back together was during a funeral. It seemed to be a harsh reality because the following year, my cousin passed away. We called her Aunt, but in reality, she was our cousin.

She and I were very close, as well; we celebrated our birthdays together. She was born June 23, and my birthday was June 22. My mother was actually her aunt, and again, there was a need for me to be there to make sure my mother was comforted. There, again, was another trip home for us to bury a loved one. That was not the end of the story. It is often said that the Lord will put no more on your shoulders than you can bear; I seemed to be finding out if this is true. I really don't know, but what I do know is that every time I stumble or fall because of some tragedy, the Lord is always there to pick me up and keep me standing tall through adversities.

Later that year, I lost another cousin. She was the sister of the one who died with my sister many years earlier. So, another trip home, another funeral service to sit through. As we moved further into that year, I got a call that my aunt had passed away. This was my mom's second oldest sister, the one whose house I stopped at every day after school to watch *Star Trek*. She, like me, was a big *Star Trek* fan, and I enjoyed stopping by her house and watching our favorite show together. There, again, would not be another house to go to and talk about the old shows that we watched together. No more holiday meals to come home to and house jump. "Lord, keep me lifted up, and continue to give me the strength to carry on"—that was always my prayer.

I really got concerned for my mother because now, she is the only living sibling left. My Aunt Hat, as we so often called her, had three girls. For the most part, they were around my mother's age—so much so that we grew up calling them Aunt when in reality, they were my cousins. Two of them had already passed away, and a few months after Aunt Hat died, my Aunt—or cousin—Linda passed away.

Linda, or Aunt Judy as we affectionately called her, was the spiritual leader of our family. When we were going through something, we would always go to her because she seemed to be the one who always knew the right things to say to keep everyone's spirits lifted. So, again, another trip home for another funeral for someone close to me.

This was another tough one because of the closeness of my cousin to me and her closeness in age to my mother. It would also mark that within a few months, my mother had lost her remaining sister and all of her cousins that she grew up with. So, comforting her was my main goal as I went home again, but by now, I was beginning to feel worn down mentally as well as physically. Who was to keep me lifted up? I supposed my wife would have; she was always great with making sure I was okay as we dealt with the losses in my family. I would hold so much in. I don't think she ever really got a clear picture as to how I was doing, but she was constantly trying.

"We fall down, but we get back up again."

Every day, there is not a storm; there are some good days, and there are some bad days. I have been blessed to have more good days than bad, and as the song says, I won't complain about a thing. I will thank the Lord for the good and the bad because I know that in the end, I will have a testimony on how much He has covered me. For the next few years, all things were well with me and my family. We had no major concerns come up, and we took every day as a blessing as we just continued to move forward with our lives. The job and family all began to have their place with me as I started to learn and realize the need for work-life balance.

In 2019, I had two surgeries on my left arm due to a tumor pressing against the nerves in my arm that caused excruciating pain. After that surgery was completed, it was discovered that the nerves in my right hand were dead. I did not have the use of my right hand. I didn't like it, but I was determined to not let it get me down, so I stayed as positive as I could.

After six months, that December, I decided to have another surgery to correct the nerve damage and to gain the use of my right hand. The tendons in my arm were moved around to connect with the tendons in my hand so that I could move my hand and fingers. The surgery was a success, and after physical therapy, I slowly regained the use of my hand. While this was going on, my baby sister had been in and out of the hospital.

She suffered from diabetes, and it had gotten to the point where it had begun to shut down some areas of her body. In addition, some areas of her body were having problems with circulation. Mine seemed to pale in importance to hers. Later that year, 2019, my sister's legs were amputated due to her diabetes—first, one leg, and then the other. She was also starting to have heart failure, and she was in a constant state of pain.

It was extremely tough seeing my sister in this state, always in pain, where nothing seems to be getting better. From that point on, the goal was to keep her comfortable and try to meet her needs as best possible. Her fiancé did his best to make sure she was taken care of.

On July 2, 2020, my baby sister Sheri died. The last sister that I will ever have was gone. As much as I thought I would grieve for my sister, I really did not. I don't know how I felt. I did care a lot, but my emotions seemed to be a little hardened, and the only concern for me was my mother. My mother had lived with my sister and her fiancé for quite a while, and being that Sheri was her last daughter, they became very close, and the loss of her hit her especially hard. She was always good at hiding her feelings, but I know she was taking it very hard. On the other hand, I was almost just going with the flow. After so much loss in the family, I kind of suppress my feelings and keep moving.

"Verily I say unto you, there be some standing here which shall not taste of death, till they see the son of man coming in his kingdom."
— Matthew 16:28

There are those times in our lives that are moments that will define who we are, what we want, and how we perceive life and the journey we take. It does not always deal with family issues or personal issues; it can be anything that has a profound effect on the way you think and act and the amount of faith you have in knowing that there is someone greater in charge of all things.

In the later part of 2015, a young lady by the name of Javona Glover walked into a store that I was managing. She was so energetic and full of life, just a happy-go-lucky young lady who was in her early twenties. When she walked into my store, she came up to me and said:

"You should hire me. I'm going to be the best employee you have."

I asked her, "How old are you? Because you look like a sixteen-year-old kid."

She just laughed and said, "I'm over twenty."

Long story short, I hired her on the spot. You know, she was right; she turned out to be one of the best employees I had. All of the customers loved her, and she got to know several of them throughout her work career. Little did I know, there were some domestic issues that she was having with a young man whom she was dating, and they also had a two-year-old daughter together.

I found out later that it had gotten to a point where he was calling the store constantly, harassing her while she was at work. My employees all did their best to make sure that I, as the manager, didn't know what was going on. On one particular day, she came in one morning wearing sunglasses, and when I told her to take them off, I could see that she had been in some kind of altercation. She said it was nothing, that she just hurt herself, but I knew better.

That morning, I told her she does not need to be in a situation that will cost her or her daughter any harm. Being in an abusive relationship does not always end well. She said he did not do anything to her, but we all knew better. Things seem to get better for the most part; I really didn't see much in the way of physical abuse after that day.

On a Tuesday morning, August 30, 2016, we began to settle into our workday. I was preparing to get on a conference call when I heard a frantic call coming from my pharmacy department. I knew it was serious by the way it was yelled over the intercom.

I was in my office with one of my team members when the call was made. Frantic, we both ran out of the office, not knowing where the crisis was. I told him to head to the front, and I would check out the pharmacy. As I got to the pharmacy, they were all sheltered in, and the department was locked up tight. They yelled for me to go to the front because Javona was in trouble. I ran to the front at top speed, and as I turned the corner, I saw the ex-boyfriend had gotten behind the counter with her.

As I got closer to the counter, it took me a few seconds for my brain to recognize that he was swinging a big knife up and down into her body. My other team member had his arms wrapped around him, but his arms were still able to get free, and he continued stabbing her. As I got to the front, the only thing I thought to do as I approached was to yell at him. I did, and by then, I was at the counter. He heard me and saw me as I was right up at the counter.

He immediately stopped! When he did, I found myself face to face with him. When he looked me in my face, he froze, dropped the knife, and ran out of the door. As people were running out of the store, I was on the phone with 911, trying to take her vitals and to check to see if she was still breathing. All of a sudden, as I looked down, I saw so much blood. It just didn't seem to stop. It was starting to run everywhere. As she stopped breathing and I was not getting any response from her, she lay there with her eyes fixed on me.

I don't know whether she was looking at me as things were happening, but her eyes were fixed on me. That is all I could see from that point, her eyes. In my mind, they pierce right through me. The look on her face in my mind says, "Jefferies, can you help me? Please help me," and there was absolutely nothing I could do about it. I was devastated. Nothing that I'd had to deal with in all of the family losses and my thirty-five years of experience at the time could prepare me for what I had just been through.

I fell back against an endcap display and just looked at her, and still, her eyes were fixed on me. At that time, the rescue squad was just getting there, and they quickly moved around me and started to work. It did not take long for them to pronounce her dead at the scene. I immediately began to call all of the necessary people. As I called our loss prevention agent to fill him in, unbeknownst to me, I was talking frantically and stating that she was dead.

He did not have a clue as to what I was saying, only that he had known me for years and it didn't sound good. He was boarding a plane in Atlanta and turned around right then, headed to his car, and came back to Tallahassee as fast as he could. I don't know how long it took him to get from Atlanta to Tallahassee, but for me, it felt like only a few minutes. Now, I was put in the position where I had to be strong for my entire store.

Everyone was crying and distraught, and I, Jefferies, had to go around and make sure everyone was all right. I had to make sure that my team received counseling and whatever help was necessary. At the same time, we were going through a major hurricane, and we had no power at work or at home. All of a sudden, I felt like a man beaten to a pulp. Who was to counsel me? Who was to make sure I was okay and still stable? All of my family was out of town, and I was there alone, at my home, in the dark, wondering if there was anything else I could have done.

I went home seeing those eyes staring right at me, and there seemed to be nothing I could do about it. As time went by, my wife often asked me to get counseling, but as a man, you know I said no to this. Perhaps I should have. Time went by, and I decided I could no longer work at that store; there had been too much at that point that I would forever be reminded of. So, a few months later, I decided to move to another store. Things that I was always concerned about at work didn't seem to matter as much anymore. Just the thought of losing someone that was young enough to be my daughter . . . The place didn't feel right anymore.

I did move to another location, but the memory of that day and the memory of her eyes remain with me to this day. It is a lot easier to deal with now because time always has a way of curing some of the things that hurt us. When I talk about it, I still get a little teary-eyed. It just shows me that somewhere deep down inside, it's still there.

I would have never thought that one of my greatest hurts would come from someone that I knew for a relatively short period of time.

There is a song that says, "We fall down, but we get up," and by the grace of God, through all of the pitfalls, the heartache, and the losses, I was able to always get back up again. To God be the glory. I will continue to keep the faith, and I will continue to walk the path the Lord has laid out for me because:

"We walk by faith and not by sight." — 2 Corinthians 5:7

Thank you, from Shirly's oldest boy, for all of the things that you instilled in me. I love you, Mommy.

Eric Jefferies

Chapter 6

HUMBLED BY EXPERIENCE

Acts 10:1–2

"10 At Caesarea there was a man named Cornelius, a centurion in what was known as the Italian Regiment. ² He and all his family were devout and God-fearing; he gave generously to those in need and prayed to God regularly." Acts 10 is my favorite Bible verse. It speaks of a man named Cornelius who was God-fearing; he was generous and strong in his faith. I have grown to understand the many similarities that I have with the Cornelius who is described in Acts 10. I hope that as you read my story, you will recognize them, as well.

I am Cornelius Williams. I was born on July 20, 1981, on a military base in Stuttgart, Germany, to Randy and Cynthia Williams. During the time I was born, my dad was in the military and was stationed in Germany. Being a military child, we moved every two to four years and lived in various cities and states. It was not until I was sixteen that we settled down in Atlanta, Georgia. Aside from the constant relocating, my childhood was pretty normal.

I took an interest in playing sports. My favorite sports were basketball and baseball. Never understood the purpose of having to move so much; never understood why Pops was always on the go. Him serving in two to three different wars and being deployed across the country sometimes had me feeling like he wasn't there and somewhat caused resentment. I remember him getting deployed one year, and I ran to hide under the bed. I wouldn't come from under the bed because I was sad and hurt that he had to leave us again.

At that young age, I did not realize he was doing it so that he could provide better lives for my mom, my sister, and me. In my early years, I was not able to build the bonds that most people have because I would meet people, make new friends, and then have to leave within two years. I feel like I was never allowed to really have solid friendships and build those solid bonds.

I remember living in Spartanburg, South Carolina, when I was thirteen to fourteen. During this time, I really started to grow close with some people. On my fifteenth birthday, we went to a party in Greenville. On the way back, one of my close friends named Mike died in a car accident. We were all drinking. I was driving one car, and my boy, Q, was driving the car Mike was in. Q wanted to race me. He hit the gas, and I fell back half a mile as I watched his car take off.

As I drove further up the road, I drove into a cloud of smoke. Their car had run into the median head-on. This moment was surreal to me. Following our instincts, we all jumped out of the car and began throwing our open beers across the median. Seeing my best friend's fifteen-year-old lifeless body slumped over the dashboard of the car really devastated me. It made me numb to death to this day. We were just getting started at an early age; we knew we would become some millionaires.

We were just hanging out and having the time of our lives, and now, he was gone. I could not wrap my fifteen-year-old mind around that. How could you be here one minute and, in the blink of an eye, gone the next minute? Within the next two months, we had to move again. That shit hurt. Not only was I beginning to build and trust someone who I considered a friend; I had to leave him dead and the memories we shared together, too.

On to the next city, next state: Atlanta, Georgia. Moving to Atlanta was so cool to me. I remember being real standoffish my first week of school, but with my character and personality, it was always easy for me to get to know people and attract the baddest females and the most popular niggas. No matter what school I attended, I was always a part of the "in crowd," but somehow, I would still feel alone.

I felt alone because I did not know who to trust, so I never allowed anyone to get close to me. I never knew if I was going to have to pick up and move again. The good thing about being in Atlanta is that I was finally closer to family, which allowed me to see them more often. This also allowed me to build a better bond with my cousins—or so I thought. Every summer and even on some holidays, we would go to Alabama and visit my grandparents and family. However, being that I did not grow up with them in my younger years, I would oftentimes feel like the outcast of the family.

Although my Pops was always on the go and not home often, when he was home, he would always chastise me. It appeared as though he only wanted to discipline me, never teach me or sit down and talk situations through with me. He missed a lot of teachable moments because discipline was his priority. He couldn't wait to pull that paddle out and whoop some ass, not understanding the reason behind some of my actions or even caring to ask me about my behavior. The crazy thing is that 99% of what I know or learned throughout life came from experience and actually going through different situations. He never sat me down with direction on how to move in any aspect of my life; everything I learned was trial and error. Looking back, I wanted more guidance from my Pops.

Being that we moved so much, I was exposed to a lot of different things, which meant I tried a lot of things. I was curious. Like most kids, I got into my share of trouble. Being curious had its pros and cons, and I was able to learn from each experience. I thank God for my momma every day; she played a critical role in me being the man I am today.

She did not raise me in a bubble; she let me learn from my mistakes and never judged me. My mom loved me unconditionally no matter what kind of trouble I found myself in. I just thank God that my curiosity didn't cost me life in prison or a death sentence.

Even though I feel like I love hard, I have always questioned if I'm actually loved by friends and family members. I sometimes question if I truly know how to love and accept love. I found myself being loyal to a lot of the wrong people, who, in return, crossed me and abused my kindness for weakness. There was a lot of jealousy, hate, and envy from one of my cousins because of who I am and who I grew to be.

My mother's side of the family is from Aliceville, Alabama, and my father's side of the family is from Cleveland, Ohio. Being that geographically, I was closer to my mom's side, I spent more time with them in Alabama. As I mentioned earlier, every summer and on some holidays, we would go to Alabama and visit my grandparents and other family members. We would rarely visit Cleveland; therefore, I did not have the opportunity to build bonds with that side of the family.

I can remember asking my mom if I could go stay with my grandmother in Alabama, and she said no because she didn't want to put that burden on her, which is why she allowed me to spend the summers there. I would stay for a few weeks. During my time there, I built a close bond with two of my cousins in particular.

We got really close, and our bond was like we were brothers. Their names are E-luv and Ball. The family thought I was so spoiled and bad, but being that I had been a lot of places, I just was hip and introduced to a lot of shit at an early age. Thank God I didn't grow up green and gullible. I shared all my experiences with my brothers from another mother and a lot of family and friends.

I jumped off the porch at an early age into things my momma and dad couldn't imagine, but it made me the man I am today. Throughout my grade school and high school years, I was an average student. I made my grades and got in my share of trouble. I believe I was acting out because I wanted my Pops around more. In high school, I dropped out in the eleventh grade and came up with the genius idea to pursue my G.E.D. After going to a few night classes, I quickly realized it wasn't for me. My mom finally let me fly, and I went to live with my grandmother in Alabama, where I graduated from high school in 2000. No one would have ever thought that I would go on to pursue college or even graduate with my bachelor's degree, but I always wanted more out of life. So, that's exactly what I did. I enrolled at Clark Atlanta University and graduated with my bachelor's degree in business management in 2006.

It was at Clark that my hustler's mentality really started to show. It started at a young age with me seeing my Pops always on the go, working and getting it in. I knew that I had to get more; the only difference between me and him was that I vowed to never leave my kids to do it. I've worked everywhere, from warehouse jobs to fast food restaurants and even call centers. I always liked money, but working multiple jobs making minimum wage is when I realized I wanted to be an entrepreneur and work for myself. It all started off in the year 2000 when I was in college.

I started selling high-end name brand watches, such as Tag-Heuer, Breitling, and Movado. I made decent money off the watches. Making fast money is what led me to take my chances at real estate. In 2001, I was in my sophomore year at CAU when I met a lady named Tracey walking on the promenade. She asked me if I wanted to make $10,000 to $15,000 by signing my name on some investment properties. Being the opportunist that I am, I said yes. At that time, I did not know I would be putting my freedom on the line for mortgage fraud and price gouging.

Eventually, I ended up buying four houses in the Oakland City community here in Atlanta, Georgia. I end up selling two and keeping two. Of the two that I kept, I was able to rent one out to tenants under Section 8. Eventually, I ended up losing that property due to lack of knowledge. I still own the last one to this day by the grace of God.

In 2004, one of my close partners and I started a company called YenFedi Ent.: Young Ellenwood Negros Financing Every Day Issues. Yen is also the Japanese currency for money. Yen also means "strong desire," and Fedi is a slang term for money. We started off rapping, and I took the role of managing. While I was in college, we started using the acronym YenFedi. We eventually ventured off into throwing parties and starting a T-shirt brand. To this day, we still stand on the brand with our day-to-day life. My partner has a successful print shop, and I finance everyday issues with my real estate. We both still strongly desire to become wealthy and provide generational wealth.

In 2014, I met my son's mother in Miami at a 2 Chainz and Jim Jones event, not knowing that one encounter would take a turn for the good and bad. We had our good and bad times, our ups and downs, but overall, we created a handsome young king. Being that

I was twelve years older than her, I often look back like, *What the fuck was I thinking?* Thinking with my *head* and not my *head*, caught up in the hype and notion that mixed women don't have attitudes like Black women. Wanting something "foreign" ended up being a life-changing experience for me.

In 2015, she got pregnant. In 2016, we had our son, and from that day, everything started spiraling downhill. With the lack of a father figure in her life, she was looking for a type of love that I wasn't mentally or emotionally signing up for. I moved her to Atlanta from Miami and introduced her to a different world, taking her to strip clubs and hanging out, and it backfired. She even ended up dancing and being a stripper.

Being around the industry, I stayed in the nightlife, in and out of clubs, and around various artists. When we would have our disagreements or she thought I was cheating, she intentionally slept with guys in my network of people to get back at me. She got real disrespectful, reaching out to close friends and family members.

In 2014, I tore my Achilles heel playing basketball. Due to how painful my injury was, doctors put me on oxycodone and Percocet. All throughout my previous years, I'd been a frequent user of Xanax and codeine. On this one particular occasion, the pills took a real toll on me that lasted for a while. I would use Percocets to suppress the embarrassment of my ex sleeping with guys in my network.

It sent me into a dark space and had me fall back from my so-called friends. I lost trust in niggas I knew for over ten years because I knew they were a part of the problem, too. Total embarrassment.

I lost weight and was sick to my stomach. Someone I gave everything to and damn near treated better than her own family crossed me out. Brought her to Atlanta after her parents put her out; gave her a home, car, and solid foundation. Now, I'm not saying I was perfect because I was not a saint, but I always stood on morals and principles, something she didn't do.

During my entrepreneurial phases in life, I've encountered a lot of ups and downs. Good and bad situations. 2014 was a hell of a year, from baby momma drama, to tearing my Achilles heel. I was still blessed enough to open a comedy club with my partner, B. We both were working hard to build it out in 2013, and our hard work was finally about to pay off—so we thought.

On opening night, we had V-103.3 broadcast live from the club. We also had a few local celebrities in attendance, such as Wanda Smith and comedian Chris Settitoff Jones. Chris was our host, and it was a successful night. We were the first ones to pay over $15,000 to bring Michael Blackson to Atlanta and to our club. We had all the major up-and-coming comedians to hit our stage. We both were learning through trial and error.

Although I'd never been in the restaurant business, B previously owned a restaurant prior to us opening the club and understood the ins and outs of the restaurant industry. He'd never been in the club life and wasn't familiar with the marketing and booking aspect. Being that I was in the nightlife for years, I had the knowledge that he lacked. It's like we were a perfect team because we were able to bring all of our knowledge and skill sets to the table and run a successful club.

Legends lasted about a year. We built that club out and tried to learn the comedy game, but it didn't go so well. We knew the comedians, and we knew the nightlife, but a comedy club is a different game. Letting our right hand know about our left hand and just not being as knowledgeable led me to reach out to the owner of the first Uptown Comedy Corner, Gary, who was well known in the Atlanta comedy world. My initial thoughts were that Gary would mentor us by supporting us and put us on game. Unfortunately, he was plotting against us the whole time. Long story short, we had a hard time getting our liquor license, and to this day, I strongly believe that he notified the county in which they shut us down. After fighting the city to obtain the liquor license and reopen a year later, guess who the new owner was? Yeah, that guy—Gary.

In 2022, I continued with my real estate journey. I started my first new construction project. Of course, like anything else we do that's new, there were ups and downs. I can admit that I made plenty of costly mistakes, such as buying wrong items, dealing with the city to obtain my permits, and having issues with tree removal. I was in a new lane and extremely green to the entire building process.

I remember us being five months into the project, and we still had not started the actual building process. I was getting discouraged because things were moving slow. I remember praying daily and asking God just to allow things to go right with this project. I desperately wanted to be successful with my first house to not only prove to myself that I could do it but to also prove it to all the naysayers. I was trying something new. It was all legit, and I wanted to leave something behind that my kids can ride past and say, "My daddy built that." I wanted to show them that we can do things differently and not do what everyone else is doing to make money. I want to leave a legacy for them.

Fast forward, the neighbor didn't want to see a young Black man successfully build a house from the ground up—and, better yet, sell it in today's market, where interest rates are high and the market is not favorable. At the beginning of the process, we crossed paths and shook hands. I would ask him what his plans were for his house and his lot. At first, he seemed like a cool guy . . . until he saw my finished product and the "for sale" sign. All hell broke loose.

The next thing I knew, I received a lawsuit letter in the mail saying I encroached on his property. The letter put me in a civil lawsuit, which potentially could have held up the sale of the house. But with prayer, God, a persistent realtor, and a hired lawyer, we continued to show the house and found loopholes that still allowed us to sell the house. I'm currently still fighting the alleged allegations out of pocket—thousands of dollars.

I know it's nothing but faith that allowed that house to sell. I still wonder why a brother with my skin color who is my age would even try to hate on my process and my success. I wonder why he would hate on the fact that I'm bringing more value to the neighborhood. I have sold the house, and I have not seen him since. Lord knows that I can not wait until we have our day in court to see how dumbfounded he looks. My God is too good to me; no weapon formed against me shall prosper.

In August 2023, I got sick and started feeling crazy pains in my chest. I had my lady friend take me to the hospital. After they ran some tests and took some labs, I found out that it was just a flu. Thank God that it was not anything major, but that day, I vowed to shake my pill habit. Over the last two years, I would pray to God numerous times a day, begging and pleading with Him to help me overcome the urges to take perks. I wholeheartedly wanted to live an addiction-free life. When I left the hospital that night and made that vow, I stuck to my promise to myself and to God. Today, I'm writing this on November 23, 2023, and happy to say I am completely clean of everything—weed, liquor, and pills. God is so good that I no longer have the urge to indulge in any of those habits. I am truly thankful to be drug-free this Thanksgiving. Lord knows it was a struggle, but by God's grace and mercy, He saw fit to give me another chance at life—a chance to finally live a drug-free life, a life of no embarrassment or shame.

I would not wish drug addiction on anybody; in fact, I will tell anyone that if the doctor prescribes you anything that can be addicting, throw that shit away. Prescription drugs are a setup, for real. I am here to tell you how good God is and that no one is too far gone that God can't save them. If God can save me and free me from all my bad habits, He will certainly, without a doubt, do the same for you. Just trust God and believe that He will show you grace and mercy, too. Nonetheless, GOD IS GOOD . . . Thank You, Sir . . .

Growing up, I was taught about God, and I definitely went to church. I mean, I went to church A LOT. It seemed as if it was mandatory to attend church. I can remember my momma made us get up early on Sundays. Not only did my mom make sure that we went to church; she also made sure that we were active in church. I can recall me and my sister singing in the choir, reciting church speeches, and participating in holiday plays. We also participated in Easter programs and even attended revivals.

Whether I really understood or not, my faith in God was embedded in me at a young age. Growing up, I remember waking up to my mother and my grandma singing church hymns. I would also hear my granddaddy sing old-school spiritual hems. Hearing my granddaddy sing really encouraged me and motivated me to learn gospel songs. To this day, I find myself waking up early and singing some of those very songs he would sing. I'm always ready to challenge people on gospel music. I will start off a song and ask my friends or family to finish the verse. Most of the time, it's a song they've never heard of. No matter who it is, I always pick a song that will stump them. I am undefeated when it comes to old-school gospel songs and hymns.

Being raised in church and having my faith rooted in me at a young age gave me a different type of faith. When I look back on life, I realize that my friends have always said I'm preaching to them or lecturing. Even now, my kids tell me the same thing. I believe that it just comes naturally from all the sermons I sat through. I have recognized that I do speak with a lot of passion, and I think that's why it may sound like I'm "preaching." Like any human, I've gone astray plenty of times, and I've had my troubled days, but I understand that God has always covered me.

As I mentioned earlier, at one point in my life, I was indulging in drugs and alcohol on a daily basis. There was even a point in my life when, for three to four years, I was totaling my cars from driving under the influence. Every time, I would hop out of the car without a scratch or a broken bone. I am not saying this to brag; I recognize the error and stupidity in my ways. My life is a testimony to how good God is. I can name countless situations that I know for a fact that GOD brought me through.

I will reiterate again that I am not a saint, and as I got older, I strayed away from the church but never lost my faith or my relationship with God. I often regret not making my children go, but lately, it hasn't been in me to attend church myself. The church, in my eyes, became judgmental, and I choose to have my own personal relationship with the Lord. A lot of people do not know that one of my favorite genres of music is gospel. I get my worship on differently by singing in the shower, singing myself to sleep, or even riding along listening to gospel music. The songs help me to connect with God.

My sobriety journey made my faith stronger, and the last couple of years post-pandemic made my faith stronger. Seeing my family members and peers suffering through the pandemic personally and on social media showed me how fragile life is. I witnessed multiple people lose their lives due to complications of having COVID-19. I also witnessed people having mental breakdowns at an alarming rate. Throughout the pandemic, I would pray and talk to God just to keep my mental state sane, thanking Him for extending me grace and mercy.

I know that it could have been me, but He kept me and gave me another opportunity to get it right. Mixing the traditional way I was taught with what life has shown me leads me to believe I'm more spiritual than religious. I will continue to give God all the glory and praise. I will continue to speak highly of God every opportunity I get. I will continue to be a better person day by day. I will continue to sing my songs.

Without faith, I don't know where I'd be. Through all my trials and tribulations, I was always taught to put GOD first. One of my favorite bible verses is Psalm 139:16, which basically says, "All the days ordained for us were written in His book before one came to be." I feel that when we're born, life is already written out on a right or wrong path. God gives us choices and allows us to make decisions. We all know right from wrong.

I thank God for my upbringing in the church; it instilled in me to pray hard, have faith, and try to live as right as possible, and everything will work out. GOD hasn't failed me yet. Yes, there are some rocky roads; yes, there have been times when I didn't understand, but I pray. I pray. I pray when it's good and when it's bad. I often wonder, *Did my momma know when she named me that I'd really have similarities to the Cornelius in the Bible?* Cornelius in Acts 10 was a good man who believed in God and always prayed.

Cornelius Williams

Chapter 7

SPIRITUAL TITAN

Baseball practice ended early, but I was ready to go home anyway, so I didn't care. I played for the Riviera Beach Braves; I was ten years old and in the fifth grade. We were supposed to get picked up from baseball practice at Tate Recreation Center by Junior's Uncle, but he never came. We made the executive decision to leave and find a phone to call my father. The barbershop was only a few blocks away, so he was able to get to us quickly to pick us up from practice. Junior's cousin stayed down the street, so we weren't that far from a phone. We got to the house and used the phone. Then, we waited.

As we waited for my father, we heard police sirens and saw flashing lights outside the living room window. Out of curiosity, we walked outside to see what happened. As we got closer to the flashing lights, we realized there was a car accident in the middle of

Australian Avenue. I was mainly in shock because I'd never seen a car accident up close.

The closer we got, the brighter and more visible the accident scene became. The cars that were involved were a police cruiser and a blue Plymouth coupe. The big coincidence is that my father owned the same type of car. I was in denial; there was no way this was my father's car. The driver's side of the car was smashed in. I refused to believe that this was real. Junior and I walked past the accident scene and towards the barbershop.

As we approached the accident scene, we saw the blue Plymouth smashed in on the driver's side with nobody in the driver's seat. We did not see any blood inside or around the vehicle, so we assumed that everybody involved was okay. Although in the back of our mind, we had thoughts about the car belonging to my father, we stayed positive. As we walked down the street, we were speaking about all of the reasons why this was not my father's car. We were in denial the whole time. The closer we got to the barbershop, the more I started feeling anxious. This is when I believe I developed anxiety. This canon event sparked a life full of anxiety stemming from my childhood to the present day.

When we arrived at the barbershop, we noticed that my father's car was gone and that the barbershop was empty. My father's barbershop was in a small shopping strip off of Old Dixie Highway. The shopping strip included a florist, a thrift store, and a BBQ spot. All the business owners knew each other, and they had an unwritten rule to look out for each other's business.

It was not uncommon for one shop owner to leave and ask another one of the shop owners to watch over their store while they ran a quick errand. When I noticed that the barbershop was empty, I went next door to the BBQ spot to speak with Mr. Bob. As I walked into the BBQ spot, I asked Mr. Bob, "Hey, have you seen my dad?" He replied, "Yes, but he left to go pick you up." At that moment, I knew something was wrong. When he told me that, my stomach immediately started hurting. I felt a very bad feeling throughout my whole body because I knew that no matter how in denial I wanted to be, I knew the car at the accident scene that Junior and I had witnessed was definitely my father's.

I called my mother and told her what happened and what Mr. B said. I'm not sure how fast it truly was, but it felt like my mom came to the barbershop as soon as I hung up the phone with her. My mom gathered my father's belongings, I grabbed my backpack, and we left the barbershop. Unbeknownst to me, that was the last time that I would ever step foot in that barbershop.

As we drove home, I was reiterating what I told my mom on the phone because although it wasn't much, I held on to the last bit of hope that my father was still alive. My mom got to the house and called my family, then took my sister to the hospital to see if it was our father involved in the crash. At 10:30 p.m., while I was waiting for my mother to return, the first person to come to my home was my grandfather. I opened the door for him. He didn't say anything; he just sat with me until my mom returned from the hospital.

Later that night, I found out that my mother ended up running into people at the hospital. As my mother was walking through the hospital, she found my father's brother, Uncle JB. My mother asked him, "Why are you here?" He replied, "Somebody told my son that James Fields was in a car accident and in the hospital at Saint Mary's." When he heard that news, he sped to the hospital because at that moment, he knew something was wrong.

This is mainly because to his knowledge, the only other James Fields in Riviera Beach was his brother. That triggered him to do his own research. (My uncle's name was James B. Fields, and my father's name was James C. Fields.) As they were waiting to hear back from the staff, a doctor finally approached them. Around 10 p.m., my mother, sister, and uncle confirmed that my father, James C. Fields, died from internal bleeding.

My sister and I were usually at odds with each other, but this night was different. When they came home from the hospital, I could tell they had bad news by the looks on their faces. As soon as they walked into the bedroom, my sister reached out to hug me. I knew at that point that if my sister showed affection like this, things had completely gone wrong. My sister and myself began to hug each other and cry because that felt like the only thing possible to do.

After I finished crying, my mom told me to take a shower to calm down. I took a shower and cried until I got it all out. When I left the bathroom, I heard multiple people in the house. Within the hour, my house was filled with family members and close family friends. Everybody rushed from their respective locations to get to our house and support us through these difficult times. As people found out what happened to my father, they began calling and coming over to provide emotional support. The night was filled with emotions and sorrow from the loss of our patriarch. At that moment, my life changed on April 11, 1996.

With my father gone, I became a man of the house. Although I was only ten years old, I had to start operating in the absence of my father. Although I couldn't provide or protect the way my father had, I had to learn about what the responsibilities included. I wanted to contribute in any way possible for my family.

As I grew older, I wondered if I was fully healed from this traumatic experience from my childhood. Unbeknownst to me, this canon event was the beginning of my future anxiety and trust issues. These issues were finally realized later in life when I went through other traumatic experiences. My anxiety has hindered me all my life. It has shown up in many ways including performance and test anxiety. People I have trust issues with include the police, loved ones, and friends. I acknowledge that I don't want to create a strong bond with people due to the fear of losing them like I lost my father—suddenly and tragically.

I didn't realize at that moment what God was doing in my life. I didn't realize that God has been creating who I am today since I was ten years old. For the longest time, I accepted blame for my father's passing. I felt that if I had not called my father that day, he would still be alive. I personally felt like it was my fault that my father was killed in that car accident. If I had never called him, he would have never left the barbershop. It took faith, maturity, and true understanding to realize that God doesn't make mistakes and that everything happens for a reason. I hated speaking about my father's passing. It made me feel very uncomfortable; that wound was bleeding, figuratively, for several years. The only way that I was able to get over that was to have faith in God and understand that His plan is bigger than whatever I could have imagined. Faith allowed me to move forward with my progression and understand that everything we go through in life is to help us and others.

Life is an amazing journey filled with triumphs, trials, and tribulations. As we move through this realm, we will be challenged by people and experiences. It is up to you to handle them accordingly. One of the things you need to have to travel this path is having faith in Christ. If you do not possess faith in Christ, your life will be difficult and confusing until you do. I've had to have blind faith in God since 1996. Without it, I was filled with fear. There are several other examples that I would like to use to display my faith in God. These examples include quitting my job after I graduated college, quitting my job during the pandemic, and healing from my divorce.

My relationship with God was started by my father. He made sure my sisters and I got dressed up and went to church every Sunday at Hilltop Missionary Baptist Church in Riviera Beach, Florida. We were in the youth choir and participated in church plays along with reciting Easter speeches. My father wanted to make sure that we were introduced to faith from the very beginning. James C. Fields III established our walk of faith, unbeknownst to us. After my father passed away—or, in traumatic terms, was killed in a car accident by a speeding off-duty police officer—I attended church with my mother at Tabernacle Missionary Baptist Church in West

Palm Beach, Florida. This was where my faith started shifting. Losing my father was such a devastating blow in my life. For a long time, I could not understand why. I could not understand why my father was killed in a car accident that I partially felt was my fault. With questions like that in my head, it forced my religious beliefs to shift from traditional to nontraditional.

When I started attending church with my mom, it was a completely different atmosphere. At my dad's church, I was accustomed to the loud organs, shouting, and dancing up and down the church aisles. The clapping and singing brought the energy to the whole production of church, but my mother's church was the complete opposite. Her church was older and more mature. I went from being in a younger church with my peers to an older church with my grandparents.

Church started at 11 a.m. and ended at 12:30 p.m. Church now lasted only an hour and a half; I was extremely happy that I didn't have to be in church all day. At Hilltop Missionary Baptist Church, the service starts at 11 a.m.—mind you, this is after going to Bible study at 9:30 a.m. Then, you stay in church until 2 p.m., just to get out of church and go downstairs to the dining hall to eat and talk for another hour. Funny thing is, there's a 4 p.m. service.

There were older people and families who went to church for Bible study at 9:30 a.m. and didn't leave until after the 4 p.m. service concluded. The super churchgoers were at church all day because on Sundays, that was their thing to do. My mother's church was less aggressive; it was very laid-back and calm. All I had to do was sit in the back of the church and let the pastor preach, then go home. I thoroughly loved going to church with my mom. It was good to have a change of church scenery.

My faith was in the process of being repaired from my fathers death, so I still wasn't fully embracing my relationship with God. Since youth, I was only taught the traditional aspect of religion. Now that I am older, the nontraditional aspect has become more fitting. In 2005, I attended a Men of Faith conference. I was an undergraduate at FAMU, and my sister told me about this conference. I am not the super religious type at all, but for some reason, when my sister told me about this conference, my discernment led me to go.

While I attended this conference, there was a message around relationships with God. This triggered me because I knew I was still unsure about my true relationship with the Lord. I did not know that I was unaware of what a relationship with God truly consisted of. After I left that conference, I realized that my relationship with Him can only be created by myself. I realized the type of connection that I wanted with Christ and how I wanted to communicate with him through prayer. Saying that Jesus is the homie is cliché, but I completely understand that statement. This is when I learned that going to church alone was not good enough; you must be in sync with Jesus Christ if you want to be his worldly follower. Now that I had established a better structure with God, I was able to operate more efficiently.

Post-conference, I changed my style of prayer when communicating with God. I transitioned from a basic list of requests to a conversation. In that conversation, I speak with God in a normal tone. I don't use any formal cadences. During these conversations, I pray for my loved ones, I pray for my enemies, and I pray for strangers. The reason why I have always wanted to include everybody possible in my prayers is because in this cruel world that we live in, there's hopefully at least one person praying for you who you know nothing about. I don't want to exclude them. This was a very pivotal point in my journey of faith in God. I now view Him as a friend and parent rather than a symbol or painting. Having faith in God allowed me to push through obstacles and tough points of my life. It is the same praying style that I use today. In my opinion, there are people who don't understand the power of prayer, and unfortunately, that's why they will never be blessed the way they wish to be blessed.

In 2009, I transitioned from a college student to an adult, from a boy to a man. During this time, I graduated from college and began working in the real world. As I graduated, I was concerned about having a job post-graduation. My degree was in political science and economics. I wanted to utilize my degree in business or in government. Since I was already working in the business world, I felt that I could use it to perform my job to the best of my ability.

At the time, I was already employed as an assistant manager at Dollar General. As graduation came near, I expressed interest in becoming a store manager. Due to me being an exceptional assistant store manager, the idea of me having my own store—within one year of joining the company!—was unanimously agreed upon amongst upper-level management. My store manager at the time was one of my biggest advocates; he made sure that I was given the opportunity to run my own store.

As time progressed, I fully embraced the job, and I had several employees on my staff. This was an interesting experience because my employees were either my same age, younger, or older. I was a twenty-three-year-old store manager; it was challenging to manage people who felt like they were your peers or that you were too young to be their manager.

I thought that I was going to stay at this job longer, but God had other plans. I had an employee who was older than me by a few years. I made her one of my assistant managers because I thought she was an exceptional employee. I later found out that was all a lie. She put on a front as if she was sweet and innocent, but she was a thief. Unbeknownst to me, this was the beginning of the end. She was leaving the store unattended on my off days and stealing from the registers. I did not know that she was doing any of this.

She was older than me, so I trusted her more than I would a younger employee, but she used that to her advantage. She was stealing deposits from the store instead of putting them in the safe. I didn't catch it at first, but eventually, I found out. Unfortunately, when I found out, it was too late. My district manager approached me and notified me of the situation. I was in disbelief at first, but after watching the camera footage, I became upset about my findings. I called a meeting with my employee and told her what I saw. She tried to deny it, but we had too much evidence, so we terminated her. Due to the negligence on my part, for not paying closer attention to what she was doing, my district manager wanted me gone, as well. He felt that I was involved with the dishonesty from my employee. He thought that I was stealing, too.

One day, I came to work, and my district manager was waiting on me. He suspended me indefinitely, pending an investigation about the missing funds. I was upset because I was making enough money to not steal, so I couldn't believe that I was being accused of it. It was December 2009; this was the wrong time to not have a job. During my suspension, I had a strong realization that God was removing this job to give me the actual occupation that I wanted and needed.

Although I was suspended, I made the decision to resign from my position as store manager for Dollar General. This was a difficult thing to do because that was my only job at the time. This is where my faith in God was tested. This is when the relationship that I started with God after the church conference was put into action. I was in a state of hurt and survival. I was good with saving money, so my bills were paid for the most part. The issue is that I didn't have enough disposable income to do things that I wanted to do. I didn't know that my unemployment would last for seven months, officially ending on my birthday weekend in July 2010.

During those seven months, I learned that I could survive off of less, and my faith in God was stronger than ever. I was at such a low point in life that I was doing odd jobs just to make ends meet. I had to humble myself because during this transition phase, I had to watch other people thrive while I was sad and unemployed. I applied to over fifty jobs during this time frame, and I received multiple letters declining my applications to various companies. I had so many letters that I was able to put them in a shoebox; I wanted to keep them as inspiration and motivation to work hard and never give up.

My faith in God was tested during these months. I had to sell my belongings in order to eat. I learned that God will only remove stuff when you have other blessings to receive. After seven months of unemployment, I finally started working again. As I began working, I realized that I had to leave my previous job in order to embrace my life as a public servant. This was the beginning of the rest of my life. I began working with at-risk kids at a nonprofit youth shelter. This became the foundation of my public service. Since then, I've worked in government and served the community through several civic organizations. Being a public servant is my calling and passion. I'm grateful for the lessons that I learned during this test of faith. God removing obstacles in your path isn't to punish you; instead, it is to bless you with new possibilities.

In 2017, I left the public sector and went to the private sector. I was working at city hall in downtown Atlanta, then I was contacted by a recruiter. That conversation led to me moving to the private sector. That is when I started working as a procurement systems analyst in IT procurement. This career transition began the next phase of my life. A new chapter had begun.

As I started working, I hated my job. I just truly did not understand it, and I didn't like corporate America at all. As I continued to work in the field, I started learning more about IT procurement. From my research, I found out how lucrative the field was. In fact, I was already doing it for the government. This was not my goal at all.

Originally, I wanted to be a government executive. I wanted to be a county administrator or a city manager. I possess a bachelor's degree in political science with a minor in economics. I also possess a Master of Public Administration degree from the University of Arizona Global Campus. My dream job is to be a nonprofit CEO, so to be working in corporate America was a complete shift in my original plan. As I gained more experience, I learned more about how the world works. You meet different people from all walks of life, cultures, and nationalities. This was the most diverse experience I have ever had in a job because normally, there are not many cultural differences. I stayed with this company from 2017 to 2020.

In January 2020, I received a promotion to their sister company. I worked in corporate America for three years and had developed the typical vision and dream of climbing the corporate ladder. I created visions in hopes that one day, I would be an executive for a Fortune 500 company. Unfortunately, that is not how the story went. As I started working on the new job, I learned about the downside of corporate America.

I'm not saying that my first job didn't have a downside, but there is no comparison to the downside I experienced in this new position. I don't want to sound cliché when I say this, but these people set me up. There's no other way to describe it. The staff that I worked with were not honest. When I began the position, I was transparent with my experience and my knowledge of the position.

They agreed that they understood. They also offered to help me in the process. In the beginning, everything seemed perfect. Later down the line, they showed their true colors.

They began to have amnesia about the agreement and attempted to hold me accountable for something that I told them I was unaware of. It was as if they were trying to force me to resign. This job started to take a toll on my mental, emotional, and spiritual health. Before I had that position, I prayed four times a day. I prayed when I woke up at 6:11 a.m., at 11:11 a.m., at 1:11 p.m., and before I went to sleep at 11:11 p.m. When I started that position, I had to turn off my alarm because my manager told me that it was interrupting my work. That is when I should have known that job was not for me.

I started having anxiety when I met with my manager. Every meeting, it felt as if she was finding a reason to bother me. I needed the job, so I didn't complain; I just internally accepted it. Although people were experiencing work fatigue during this time, I didn't think I was in that number. In February 2020, everything seemed fine. I noticed some people started coughing and getting sick, but I assumed it was their allergies due to it being close to the spring season. I remember being in my home and getting sick.

I thought it was seasonal allergies, as well, so I never questioned it to be anything else. As I went to work, I saw more people getting sick, coughing, and having to go to the hospital. I knew something was wrong, but I didn't know what it was. I started hearing about this disease that made everybody sick called the coronavirus. I was unaware of what it was and what it was able to do. All I knew was that I did not want to get it.

In March 2020, I woke up on a Tuesday morning as if it was a normal day. I got in my car and drove to QT to get some gas and a chocolate cappuccino. As I was leaving the gas station to get on Interstate 675, I got a phone call from one of my managers. She told me that we would be working from home indefinitely and not to come into the office. She then told me that it was because we were shutting down due to the coronavirus spreading and that we must maintain a safe distance to help stop people from contracting the virus. At first, it felt perfect, but as time went by, it was worse than before.

The relationship with my management continued to get worse. I finally accepted that they did not want me to work with them anymore. The red flag and the smoke signal that they gave me to confirm they didn't want me working there anymore was when one of my managers would never help me when I had issues at work. There was a task that I did not know how to complete and I needed her help with, but she always found a way and a reason not to work with me. When I realized that, I knew it was time to go. As time progressed throughout the year, working from home felt more like pain than pleasure. I did not enjoy work anymore. I began to hate everything about it. Every time I met with my manager, my anxiety skyrocketed. Every Sunday before I went to work, I'd get the Sunday blues. It was time to go. One day, I was in a meeting with my manager, and I finally had enough. I was ready to quit.

The next day was when I established a higher level of faith in God. I prayed to God for an answer. After I spoke to God and He reassured me that everything was going to be okay, I called my managers and told them that I quit. My career at that company started in March 2017 and concluded in November 2020. After I quit that job, I had some of the hardest days that I have ever experienced in my life. As I was sitting in my apartment by myself, I couldn't help but overthink about my life.

I questioned everything, and I was very unsure. The healing process and self-realization process are some of the toughest processes to ever go through. When you live by yourself, you're forced to face yourself, and you're forced to accept your flaws. I had to reinvent myself. I had to figure out who I wanted to be moving forward.

I began therapy along with working on my physical health. I exercised daily; it helped my thoughts flow. I prayed every day, all day. My faith in God was stronger than it had been in years. The more I trusted God, the more my life flourished. A minister told me that you must sit still to hear the general's voice. The general is God. If you remove all the outside noise, you will be able to hear God's voice. God speaks straight to you through many channels and many people. There are ministers everywhere you go, not just in the pulpit. God isolates you to protect you. During this period of isolation, I learned exactly the man I wished to be.

This period of life was very challenging, mainly because I forced myself to be extremely disciplined. This was the first time in my entire life that I ever challenged myself. In March 2021, I was ready to reenter the workforce. I had a strong planning session in which I tried to structure how I wanted my future to look. I started looking for jobs and speaking with recruiters.

At first, I wasn't able to find anything, so I started to get discouraged. Finally, I received a phone call from a recruiter, who told me that a medical device company wanted to hire me. I was unemployed for six months, and God never allowed me to go without. God allowed me to have increase, God allowed me to heal, and lastly, God allowed me to become the man I am today. I was unemployed from November 2020 to March 2021. Without God, there is no way that I would have made it to where I am today.

Jared Fields, MPA

Chapter 8

Unveiling Faith: Lessons from the Journey

A preacher posed a question once: "What happens when your dreams turn into nightmares and monsters start to show up?"

Matthew 21: 18-19

Early in the morning, as Jesus was on his way back to the city, he was hungry. Seeing a fig tree by the road, he went up to it but found nothing on it except leaves. Then, he said to it, "May you never bear fruit again!" Immediately, the tree withered.

In God's eyes, the time that we live on earth is only a vapor of time, a short period, and our life vanishes away. I believe that God requires us to bear fruit. I interpreted the above verse as us making use of our life and producing fruit. Because the fig tree was not producing fruit, Jesus sped up the process to wither since it did not produce. I believe that we are here to produce and live out our dreams because if we don't, we will wither quickly.

I hope to turn my short stay here into a fruit-producing forever with my story for my family and legacy. I hope to inspire, guide, and teach what I have gained in the physical and spiritual form. I hope to specifically touch my brothers and sisters who look like me. I also hope to touch the brothers and sisters who do not look like me. Overall, I hope my story brings light and serves as inspiration.

I believe that my journey so far is unique and different from your average African American stereotype. Okay, okay, okay—so, here are the ones that are true for me: Yes, I grew up in a single-parent home. Yes, I barely know my father. Correct again—I grew up in the inner city, Black middle-class, and some will still call this the ghetto depending on what side you are standing from. Great, I'm glad that you know my life already, ha! But sincerely, I hope that my journey can add to your journey.

I often go back to my collection of memoirs as a reference. I've faced lions, lived in the jungle, and had my share of challenges with health—but I'm still here. And I'm not alone: God has been with me every step of the way. And when times were tough, He was right there beside me, helping me through it all. And sometimes, I did not believe He was there.

I've also tussled with God while I was in sickness and contemplated what side of the fence I should be on. We tussled because I wanted to know why God let bad things happen to good people. I am learning that God will give you what you pray for, but He will do so in a foundational way.

When you ask for strength, you may experience a burden. When you ask for patience, you may experience something that will force you to grow your capacity in patience. And sometimes, GOD may send some circumstances your way because HE knows you will need the experiences for the things He intends to bless you with. And now, I've started to break the cycle of codependency, and I'm learning to trust God more than ever before. And I know that if I stick with Him, He'll never let me down!

Last, my story is a journey of love. Navigating love as a man—and as a Black man—is not easy. Sometimes, to dig deep into a subject like love, we must turn the mirror on ourselves. It's not easy, but we must act. If you don't have the courage to act, life will move on without you. I hope that maybe some of my journey will let you know that you are not alone in yours.

I am Corey Hackett, and here are some brief inserts of my life through the lens of my soul. The lessons I have learned have helped me develop, nurture, and birth my faith.

*Journal inserts are bold, dated, and italicized.

Facing Fear in the Lion's Den
Summer of April, 2000

I always liked the smell of freshly cut grass in the summer at a young age. My oldest brother had just finished cutting the grass, and it was a perfect time for me to wash my motorcycle bicycle I had gotten for Christmas. The bike was like one of those Kawasaki Ninja bikes but with pedals. I was only allowed to ride, like, a ten-block radius in my neighborhood. Dixie Hill, an apartment complex, was equivalent to the elephant graveyard in The Lion King, the dark, shadowy place. Dixie Hill was not all bad, but for a young teen with a motorcycle bike, it's like being the perfect prey for a carnivore in a jungle.

Every now and again, these carnivores will walk from Dixie Hill to West Lake Station. Our house was in between. On this beautiful summer day, I crossed paths with Leon, a.k.a. Scar. Leon was a person you never wanted to cross because no light ever shone from him. He had to be nineteen to twenty-two years old at the time, while I was only thirteen. "Lil Corey, let me ride that bike, bruh!" Out of fear and with no hesitation, I had let Leon ride my bike. I did not want any trouble. He rode around in cycles and popped a couple of wheelies. I just knew he was going to take off with my bike. Leon came to a stop and got off the bike. "That's a nice bike, lil bro."

As I proceeded to take my bike, Leon asked if I wanted to play karate. I'm pretty sure I did not say yes, but somehow, he ended up roundhouse kicking me in the face. I knew then I was in a real fight because play . . . play did not feel like this. I heard a ringing in my head, and he encouraged me to "play" back. Honestly, can I even call this a fight? I don't remember getting a lick off. He beat the shit out of me doing karate. After my ass-whooping, I remember running home to get my brother. I can't quite remember what he said, but it wasn't encouraging or helpful. On that night, I did my first couple of push-ups by choice. I would not get my ass whooped like that again.

"Fight Back! Prepare for Battle to Protect Your Legacy and Family!"

This fight is woven in the fabric of my being, as it was probably my first real fight where I felt pain and felt that someone really wanted to hurt me. The experience taught me very valuable lessons in life. I realized that I needed to learn how to protect myself from real harm and/or how to prevent it. It's one thing to spar and play fight with siblings, but what happens in a situation when you are cornered? I also learned what taking an L felt like. I believe one or two things can help when you take an L. You can hit rock bottom and let that experience keep you down, or you can learn and grow stronger from it. You can either become familiar by way of contentment, or you can look at it as a springboard or a foundation to build upon. Les Brown once said, "If you fall, be sure to fall on your back because if you can look up, you can get up!" Becoming content with being at the bottom is not a good thing. And if you feel stuck, I encourage you to look up. I encourage you to seek and find that little speck of light and optimism. And when you do, I want you to focus and double down on that positive thought.

When we are faced with adversity and affliction, our character develops. We may not even realize that the way we react to our challenges is shaping us into who we are. Our reactions can be positive or negative, but either way, we are learning about ourselves and how we react to certain situations. It's important to remember that there's no such thing as a perfect person. We all have flaws—but those flaws make us who we are.

If you're looking for character development, adversity and affliction are not your only options. You can develop your character in many ways. Your own personal experiences can help you to grow as a person, and you don't need to go through something traumatic or dramatic to get there. It's more about how you deal with those experiences and how you respond to them. A lot of things are not new under the sun, but what sets us apart is how we respond to them. How we respond to a thing will sometimes dictate the next decade of our lives. How we respond will show us where we are rooted. Are we responding from lack, hurt, and pain? Or will we respond from resilience, strength, and faith?

Graduation and the Concrete Jungle
May 2010

I received this journal on May 1, 2010, as a graduation gift. Today, I am not afraid to fill the pages with words. I didn't know how I wanted to begin, but now, I realize that I want to fill the pages with life because I will look back on these experiences and hopefully grow from each experience.

May 16, 2010, Morning

Brooklyn, New York

Yesterday was the official start of my new beginning, although every day is the beginning of the rest of my life. I graduated May 1, 2010, from Albany State University in Georgia with a B.A. in Mathematics. After graduation, I spent a week in Albany, Georgia, then another week in Atlanta, Georgia, before I landed in the concrete jungle, New York City. They say that this is the place where dreams are made reality, but right now, my mind is focused on finding my purpose and building a relationship with God.

When I hit the ground running in NYC, I was excited and terrified at the same time. I believe that sometimes, the unknown can be some of the best motivation. I had given myself about two weeks to find a job, and if I did not, I would move back to Atlanta. I probably would've done what I thought was safe—still an interest, but safe because it felt familiar because it was what I saw as a child. I am sure I would've been a traditional teacher, a lawyer, or a police officer.

I was encouraged as an adolescent to think about a respectable career, something I could retire in and have a great pension, but times have changed. Growing up, I saw male teachers, mechanics, police officers, postmen, and barbers. And, of course, I saw doctors, lawyers, and judges. I could see how my life would look, especially being down in Atlanta. However, I loved to dress up and help people become a better version of themselves even at a young age. I wanted to work in fashion, and by the time I was in college, I knew I needed to leave the nest to do it.

I had one suit that I could still wear out of college. It was black. I wore that suit for almost a week straight until I found a job. My sister had given me the road map on where the high-end stores were on Fifth Avenue, Madison, and in SoHo. I was green, and I don't think that was a bad thing because I think too much influence can take you away from your truth or sponsoring thought. I threw on my suit with a few resumes in hand, and then I was off to make my dreams come true.

I walked into the corporate office of Ralph Lauren because in my mind, that's where I needed to go to get a job from Ralph Lauren. I remember approaching the desk of the secretary. "Hi; how can I help you?" she asked. I asked for the CFO at the time, and the secretary was prompt about checking to see if she had any availability. I believe this only happened because of the suit that I had on. The fit of the suit was proportional to my body. The style was a notch lapel, two-button, straight pocket, double-vented classic. I am sure she thought I was someone important, not knowing I was a green, southern graduate from Atlanta who was about to ask if they had any opportunities. To my surprise, Robin came out immediately because I believe the secretary had said, "Corey Hackett is here to see you." She came out and quickly gave me a look, turned to the secretary, and started to instruct her on how to look at her calendar.

Clearly, I was not on her calendar, and apparently, the secretary was new. See, God is always working. Robin then quickly came over to shake my hand, introduced herself, and told me to follow her into her office. She asked how she could help me, and I told her that I was a recent graduate from Albany State University in Georgia, and I was looking for a stylist opportunity with Ralph Lauren. I did not have any fashion retail experience, as I had only worked in the fast- food industry and as a tutor in college.

After a few lines back and forth, Robin picked up the phone and made a phone call. When she hung up the phone, she looked at me and said, "Corey, it was refreshing to meet you." She had told me to go to the 57th & Fifth Avenue Club Monaco, ask for Kelly, and tell her that Robin sent me. And this is how I started my fashion career in the concrete jungle, New York City.

My method was super unorthodox, but I did the thing I thought would set me apart. My mentors and professors had me convinced that the workforce was super competitive, and I would need to figure out a way to stand out. I was afraid and green, but at the same time, I was fearless. Being afraid made me fearless. Sure, I could've applied online like everyone else, but then that would put me in the pool with my competitors, so I decided to create a path.

"There is no competition. You just have to be more creative, live the truth in your mind, and not follow the crowd."

June 28, 2010, Monday

It's been about thirteen days since I last wrote, so here is an update. I received my first paycheck from Club Monaco in Manhattan. I was called in for training at the Therapy Wine Bar in Brooklyn. My best friend got married on the 26th of June, and they are also expecting. I spent some time with Portia, and I might have the opportunity to work a salary-based job while I am in New York, as well.

Greg's wedding brought me to a new mindset and has given me a new motivation in life. I am proud of him, and I pray that God blesses his family and that HE guides them to a fulfilling and everlasting future.

Being in New York for a month has given me this sense of urgency to be the best me I will be. Only possible with God. Thank You, Father! This week, I will be the best me I can be and stay open to whatever God brings my way. Love You, God, and thank You in advance . . .

I believe that sometimes, taking the road less traveled makes the story interesting. It's almost like working out, in a sense. When you do the first rep, it feels odd, and you notice the muscles you haven't used in a while. But by the third set, you feel stronger and more comfortable with the exercise.

I also believe that when we take a risk, whether it be physical or emotional, we are opening ourselves up to potential growth. The more risks we take, the more opportunities there are for us to learn about ourselves and grow as human beings. This can be both exciting and terrifying at times. I believe that if we don't push ourselves outside of our comfort zones, then we won't ever fully understand who we are as individuals. We may not understand what our potential might be as people living in this world. Find a community of risk-takers, stay close to people who feel like sunshine, and don't be afraid to be a light for those who need sunshine, too. There is nothing wrong with doing it the traditional way. Honestly, there is no wrong way if both ways can work. In situations like these, I don't think there is a wrong answer. I believe if you believe in yourself, no matter what your decision is, God will start to maneuver when you begin to move. The important thing is that you move!

"Take the road less traveled."
"When you move, God will maneuver."

I was afraid of taking the road less traveled. I was afraid that it would be too hard or that I wouldn't be able to do it. But then, I realized that if I didn't take the road less traveled, I'd always wonder what if. Most importantly, I was not afraid of failing or taking an L; I had done that with Scar.

Sometimes, the map won't appear until you start to move, and sometimes, God won't start to maneuver until you start to move. So, if you're in a place where you're wondering whether it's time to take a leap of faith, my advice is this: Don't wait too long to make a decision.

If you don't take the road less traveled when given the opportunity, then one day when you look back on your life, you might wish that you had done so then—and wondered what might have happened if only.

> *"Don't go where the path may lead,*
> *but go to where there is no path, and leave a trail."*

Battling Health Challenges
July 7, 2014

After being out of work for two weeks, I finally mustered the strength to go back. Monday, the longest day of my life. Two weeks prior began the flare-up. My joints became weak. Abscesses and fistulas appeared near my bottom, which made it hard for me to walk and sit down. At night, I had cold sweats, trying to figure out a comfortable position to rest. At the point of the flare-up, anything that enters my body is critical to the healing process. Every two days, I was in a drugstore to buy Johnson & Johnson non-stick pads so that my bottom stayed as clean and dry as possible because of drainage. After losing a couple of pounds, I had to change my wardrobe to fit my new body type.

I woke up at my sister's apartment in Bed-Stuy, Brooklyn. She went to Atlanta for the Fourth of July weekend. I used her apartment for her deep tub. I soaked in Epsom salt to heal and take the soreness from my body. I woke up weak and moving slowly. The first thing I reached for was a bottle of water to jump-start my body.

I received wake-up calls from Tatia and my roommate, Kyle, because I was afraid of not waking up on time. This is what I told them, but I was really afraid of not waking up. I walked over to the tub and began running water. I prayed for strength to make it through the day. It would be the first day in two weeks that I would function for eight hours under stress and on my feet all day. But if I didn't push, I would never get better. After soaking for about thirty minutes, I lay on the sofa to collect my thoughts and build my confidence. I began to put on my clothes while packing my bag. I made sure I had bottled water and a home-cooked, organic meal. I had a friend cook for me because I was too weak to stand and cook. Before I left, I had to take Angel out to pee. As soon as I started down the stairs, my body began to sweat all over. I became dizzy, but I continued to push through. On the train, I believe I had an anxiety attack because I felt crowded, hot, and faint, but I managed to push through until 59th Street–Columbus Circle from Utica on the A line.

I only had one pad left entering work. I knew that at some point, I would have to go to the drugstore to get more, along with baby wipes to clean the area before replacing the medical pad.

As I limped into the store, moving slowly, people were asking if I was okay. They asked if I would make it, and they were happy to see me— "You lost weight!", "What happened?", etc. Now, my day begins at H&M as a department manager who pretty much manages the entire store. Some of the staff thought I should go home because I moved and looked weak. But after two weeks, I at least wanted to try and show my true condition for job protection because I still had haters who wanted my absence to be a lie.

Every half hour after going to the drugstore, I was in the restroom refreshing myself. I was in pain off and on. I considered going home, but I continued to push once I got to the halfway mark and after a little encouragement from Tatia. I needed lunch badly because I could feel my energy leaving me. After I ate, I walked outside a little bit and reached out to some doctors in Atlanta for referrals because I would never go to a public hospital again.

My sister had taken me to a public hospital because I was in so much pain. Once we arrived and they put me in the waiting room, I was horrified at what I had seen. I prayed to God to use me or take me because I was prepared to die. I would rather have suffered than let anyone in that hospital touch me.

After lunch, I felt a little better, but I was in pain from being on my feet for so long from being down for weeks. So, I mentally planned out the rest of my day so that time would be accounted for. Good thing I had the next day off because I know I could not have done two days back-to-back after the initial comeback. When 8 p.m. struck, I was making my exit, straight to my sister's house to get in the tub to soak. After I got out of the tub, I literally could not walk. I was forced to retire early, although that's all I wanted.

The moment my sister brought me through those hospital doors in Brooklyn, I knew I had entered hell on earth. The waiting room was pure chaos—people bleeding, screaming in agony, stretched out on gurneys in the hallway with nowhere to go. It was like a scene from one of those '90s ER movies. My heart sank, and I prayed, "God, use me or take me, because I'm ready." I was prepared to die before I let anyone in that place lay a finger on me.

I turned to my sister and said, "Let's get out of here now." She didn't argue. On the way home, I remembered the book that had saved my life once before—*The Maker's Diet*. For the next two months, that book became my bible. It lays out a spiritual forty-day diet engineered to heal the body through food and prayer. I vowed to follow it to the letter, trusting it would restore me to health once more through the power of God. The journey would not be easy, but I was determined to see it through.

"Your 'Why Me?' Will Help You Discover Your Why"

The butterfly is an amazing creature that has four stages in its life cycle. First, an egg is laid by a female butterfly, which then hatches as a larva. This stage is also known as a caterpillar because it is the only stage where the larva has legs. After eating and growing larger as a caterpillar, it sheds its skin and hardens into a pupa, or chrysalis. The pupa is also referred to as a cocoon because it protects the pupa from predators and environmental conditions that would harm the butterfly during its developmental stage.

As the caterpillar develops in the cocoon, it will begin to break through the cocoon. Now, this breaking will seem painful to the human eye, but it is necessary. It's necessary for the butterfly to build strength overall and to build strength in its developing wings. The caterpillar will fight and fight to get out. It will struggle, it will stop and start again, but it will not stop until it is fully out of the cocoon. If those wings do not develop, then the butterfly won't be able to maneuver or survive in its environment against prey.

The caterpillar's struggle is a necessary crucible. Though we may see its striving and feel moved to ease its pain, we must stay our hands and know it's developing, for it is only through the fire of great effort that the caterpillar will transform into a butterfly, gaining the strength and fortitude to spread its wings.

Intervening to end the struggle early might seem merciful but would only cripple the emerging butterfly. Without the challenge to fully build its wings, it would never gain the power of flight. Without the resistance to strengthen its muscles, it would languish earthbound and vulnerable.

The caterpillar's labor pains are the growing pangs of a creature forged through adversity. Just as the twisting, writhing caterpillar must force its way out of the unyielding cocoon, we too must embrace the struggle to reach our highest potential. The butterfly's splendor is only possible after the caterpillar's strife.

The butterfly's splendor is only possible after the caterpillar's strife.

So, we must allow the caterpillar's transformation to proceed unimpeded, no matter how difficult it is to watch, for only through the crucible of intense effort will the caterpillar gain the strength and abilities it needs to live fully as a butterfly. Our highest selves are realized when, like the butterfly, we push through challenges that demand everything we've got. The caterpillar's struggle is sacred. Honor it, and in time, vibrant wings will emerge.

When I was a child, I would often ask God, "Why me?" I struggled with the idea of transformation. It's not that I didn't want to be a butterfly—I just didn't understand why it had to be so painful. Many times, I became frustrated by the process and wondered if it was worth it in the end. I wanted it to stop. I thought about pulling the plug a few times. I would write angrily to God in my journal. I wrestled with God and His word at times.

It took some time, but I began to see what my struggles were building within me: strength. And as I grew into adulthood, I realized that this process is necessary for us all. Not only does it build strength for what we may encounter ahead; it also teaches us how to trust in the suffering as we survive through it. Bishop T.D. Jakes said that sometimes, the understanding and learning will come in retrospect. He said to not ask God why you are going through something; just focus on getting through it. Focus on surviving that thing. And when you do survive it, God will reveal why you have gone through it.

Maybe your pain builds strength for you. Maybe your pain and hurt have prepared you for your next chapter. Maybe those failures made you more empathetic to others. And maybe, just maybe, after you survived a valley point, it gave you ultimate confidence and true faith in God. Sometimes, operating with a lack or a weak mindset can take you toward a downward spiral. As people, it is easy to always focus on the negative, especially if we get caught up in a negative cycle. But my journey has taught me that God focuses on your strengths. Don't ignore your strength, and don't waste your hurt!

"Don't waste your hurt."

Breaking the Cycle of Codependency
1/16/15

Trying to figure this out. Trying to figure out why I constantly do things over and over again. Why do I keep catching myself in the same cycle? What is God trying to tell us? What is the Universe trying to teach? What are we creating consistently but don't know we are creating, repeating creation? We love, then destroy, then love again. They love you, then they hate you, then they love you again.

We are all trying to figure this out. Trying to figure out why we keep doing the same things over and over again. Why do we keep catching ourselves in the same cycle? What is God trying to tell us? What is the Universe trying to teach us? What are we creating consistently but don't know we are creating, repeating creation? We love, then destroy, then love again. They love you, then they hate you, then they love you again.

We find ourselves caught up in a cycle of pain and suffering, not knowing how to stop it all. We find ourselves in relationships with people who make us feel loved but then hurt us so badly that it causes us more pain than happiness. The funny thing about it, though, is that when they treat us like crap, we still want them back because they treated us so badly that it becomes normal. We can do a thing well and become good at it, and we can do a thing wrong and become good at it.

This kind of behavior is called codependency, and it's a form of addiction. It's just like drugs or alcohol, where someone else's actions control your life rather than your own decisions or experiences from childhood, past relationships, or maybe even current ones.

I believe that we need to learn how to take responsibility for our own lives instead of allowing others around us to dictate what happens next based on their own needs and/or experiences. The cycle that keeps happening repeatedly is the thing that we need to focus on. This very cycle is the period when we should lean into our faith and do the work. If we do so, it will enable us to move forward to the next level, to the next checkpoint, and to the next chapter of our lives. As frustrating as this is, our "Why me?" will help us discover the *Why* on our paths to greatness.

Create a place before people. Create a place for who and what you want. God prepared a place long before He created us. Then, He put us in it. After my continuous cycles, this became clear to me. It was difficult for me to fully be present with someone if I was not at a point I was comfortable with myself. Be aware of your needs and how you are loving yourself before putting people in your world.

"Create a place, and then put people in them."

"It's the nature of people to love, then destroy, then love again that which they value most." — God

"All human actions are motivated at their deepest level by one of two emotions: fear or love."

Embracing Faith in Sickness
July 5, 2014

Sickness has grabbed hold of my body once more. I am currently living in New York City. The holistic lifestyle I am supposed to be living is very complicated to maintain.

Because I had been down this road before, I knew exactly how to respond. I also came to the realization that nothing really matters if your health is not good. You can't take care of or be there for the people you love if you don't take care of yourself. I was living the dream in NYC, but I was lacking the discipline with my diet, routine, and awareness to root in my dreams. I took this as a warning sign that my lack of discipline would turn my dreams back into a nightmare.

All or Nothing: A Lukewarm Life No More
4/2011

Revelation 3:16

"So because thou art lukewarm and neither hot nor cold, I will spew thee out of my mouth."

I can't live my life lukewarm anymore. All or nothing. Take me, Lord; use me, Lord; heal me, Lord, God. In Jesus's name, I pray . . .

You must decide! You can not be lukewarm in anything you do because the laws of God and the Universe do not operate in confusion. Our dreams are attached to our destiny, and I believe that God has a dream that He wants to give to everyone's life. But we must choose to lean into that dream 100%. We must not be lukewarm.

I did not lack dreams, but I lacked discipline with my diet. My diet lacked in a way that affected my dreams in a negative way. If I continue to lack discipline, it will ultimately affect my destiny. It would aid in creating another cycle in my family lineage around health and diet. We must not be lukewarm!

Discipline is hard. It's the hardest thing you'll ever do, and sometimes, it will feel like you're failing at it. But I want you to know that the discipline is there for a reason: to make sure that your dreams don't die.

It's easy to give up when things get tough—I've been there. I know how it feels like to have the wind knocked out of your sails, or even worse, when those sails have been torn off completely by a storm. But when we lean into our discipline and work on our destiny, we can build a stronger foundation for ourselves and our dreams.

And I promise: If you keep leaning into your discipline, one day, you'll wake up and realize what an amazing person you are, with a life that is beyond anything you could have imagined before. We are not lukewarm!

Induced Labor of Love
4/5/2015

Induced labor is when a doctor gives you medicine and uses other methods to start your labor. The problem is that sometimes, when labor is induced, the product and/or babe is not fully developed.

I've noticed that when I first involve myself with a woman, I give my truth and emotions. When I give the woman the very thing she needs and asks for, it's like I somehow call her bluff. There is usually an excuse or someone in her past that holds her back. It becomes confusing because we have the first conversation about relationship expectations with discernment. It's obvious that whatever is holding her back wais not meeting her expectations. So, why is there a delay in moving forward? While I give time for the woman to figure out her situation or cut ties, I am still upright, giving love, affection, and transparency. I can admit that at moments, I do receive in return, but nothing 100%. I often question our state and/or title with our situation because I am anxious and feel like no progress is being made, only steps backward.

Now, the induced labor starts. I become more vocal about what I want. Full love received with conflict or contention. Then, boom! It happens. The time I spend giving love fades because I am now insecure about her past because of the time frame. The time spent trying to cut ends is time missed in development. The tables somehow turn, where I start to not care because I feel like my value was taken for granted. After three months spent cutting a loose end, she is now ready to give me her full attention and love. But at this point, I am all out of love to give because of uncertainty. And even now, I begin to distrust this initial thought about being serious . . . Lord, I need therapy.

Now, I am no psychologist, but I am sure the way we show up in relationships or how we deal with love has a direct relationship with our families, our environments, and how we received love over a period of time. Over experiences, I have learned this: Do not force love. If we induce that labor, we may lack the strength to handle the tough things down the road.

The majority population gives into the attitude of "love at first sight"; a look here, a smile there, and a few interactions later, we are in love. In reality, this is not love; it's lust, infatuation, or a strong case of loneliness. The true feeling of love does not discriminate by looks; it must be carefully nurtured over time by learning how to love oneself first, then loving someone else. We must decide on this paradigm of thinking.

Love Is a Decision

My experiences and my walk with God continuously shaped my definition of love. My experiences in my past relationships have taught me a lot about myself and shaped how I see myself. I believe that love makes allowances for people's weaknesses and covers a person's faults. I have been in situations where we said, "I'll love you as long as you never hurt me or as long as you never make a mistake." That's too much pressure and unfair to the other person. I have learned to be a person who shows mercy even in advance of a mistake or a wrong action rather than flaunting someone's failure

because God never does that to us. I believe that love is service to others and to yourself. Love will refuse to let you stay in your incomplete state. Love is a decision.

Conclusion

A preacher posed a question once: "What happens when your dreams turn into nightmares and monsters start to show up?" You wake up and begin to live! Every experience is an opportunity to exercise or respond positively or negatively. Sometimes, taking an L means taking a *learning*. Pain and hurt can be generated into positive energy to achieve your goals fearlessly. This can be caused by heartbreaks in relationships and/or family hurt. Learn from your experiences, grow from these experiences, and become a better person in life because of your experiences.

Sometimes, you just need to live your truth, create your own path, and trust that gut feeling. That gut feeling, I believe, is God talking to you, a subtle push in the right direction. Follow that intuition. God works most when we see it least. So, don't get discouraged just because you don't see anything happening in your life. When things are looking bleak and it feels like there is no way out, focus on something positive. Dream that positive dream more vividly, and deal with the thing you need to be disciplined in. Just because God shows you dreams in your dysfunction does not mean He is going to give it to you in dysfunction. He wants to show us what we can have.

Remember, there is no wrong choice when making a positive decision. As long as you are willing to do all that you can do and see it through, you will reach your destination. But you can not be lukewarm! You must decide! Discipline will aid in our hope. Hope is the positive expectation in any circumstance. Look for something good when everything around you is going bad. That hope will aid in our FAITH because when we begin to move with purpose and pure hope, I believe that GOD will maneuver. Last, I want you to remember to love. Remember that love is action, and if you are doing it right, it will demand a positive response. Love is a decision; it is both practical and emotional. My story is a reminder that life is not always easy and that we may encounter "monsters" and obstacles along the way. But we can choose to face these challenges with resilience, determination, and faith, using them as an opportunity to learn, grow, and inspire others.

Corey Hackett

Chapter 9

Proof Is in the Progress

Focus On the Now

I have never been one to brag, but for the sake of making a point, I am going to right now. To begin, I am a community development consultant based in Atlanta, Georgia, and would consider myself a pretty good one. I have been blessed to lead a great number of organizations and projects over the years that provide wonderful impact to the community abroad.

One organization I would like to shout out is The 400 Legacy Project, located in the city of Philadelphia and dedicated to creating model communities whose missions are focused on setting the precedent for the next 400 years. Through this endeavor, we were able to get a resolution passed in the city of Philadelphia, making the last Monday of February W.E.B. DuBois Day and working to establish the day in Accra, Ghana.

Another organization I would like to highlight is The Black Excellence Society, formerly known as For(bes) The Culture, a network established to create equitable pathways for Black and brown professionals. I have the opportunity of sitting on the board for three non-profits, Crystal Stair Group, The Cheaux Love Project, and Atlanta For Haiti. Each of these organizations work with youth, providing the resources they will need to better their future.

Lastly, I help facilitate a great mentorship initiative with the Obama Foundation's My Brother's Keeper Alliance, titled Big Brothers Anonymous, which works to provide positive resources to young boys of color ages twelve to twenty-four who are affected by high social determinants such as high expulsion rates, high incarceration rates, high STD rates, and high numbers of single-parent households.

Everything mentioned above holds a dear place in my heart but does not make me who I am. I can recall the state of mind I was in before collaborating with each of those endeavors and the adversity I dealt with mentally from the grief of losing loved ones and just going through the ups and downs of life. Despite how beautiful the experience of my career has been, my life's mission has always been tested and tried. Maya Angelou said, "You may encounter many defeats, but you must not be defeated. In fact, it may be necessary to encounter the defeats so you can know who you are, what you can rise from, and how you can still come out of it."

Adversity can either make you or break you. In my case, it has made me and is still making me. A day doesn't go by when I don't acknowledge my loved ones who have gone on to be with the Lord. The feeling is like they moved to a different country, and all I can do is write a letter to communicate with them. Though they are not here with me physically, I know I am connected with them spiritually, and that has been enough.

My family, friends, and colleagues have always told me to share more of what I do with the masses. They believe that I have so many great things to say, and I can honestly say that I think they're right. God has blessed me with an experience that can inspire millions the same way it inspires me and those I care about. Bragging to myself has always been easy for me.

I'd talk to myself for hours about how God was doing great things in my life despite the adversity I experienced, but I would still struggle to share with others what God was telling me. In some ways, I felt that I was not worthy enough to share my knowledge or that I may have not completed what God called me to do. Nevertheless, God has always been there, watching over me and making sure that His glory shines whether I share or not.

My prayer is that those who read this chapter understand that God has always been with you, He is with you now, and He will be with you no matter the circumstances. He says in His word, "Trust in Him, and lean not to your own understanding; in all your ways acknowledge Him, and He shall direct your path." I trusted God during those tough times, and He led me to great opportunities. He placed visions in my head and spoke to me through dreams and people, encouraging me to keep my mind stayed on Him and the calling He placed on my life. If you are in a tough place right now in life and you don't know what to do, I recommend being still, calm, and aware of where God has brought you.

The Dip

Best-selling author Seth Godin wrote an amazing book that changed my life years ago titled *The Dip*, where he proves that winners are really just the best quitters. He shows that winners quit without guilt until they commit to beating the right Dip. Every new endeavor begins fun but then becomes challenging and not fun at all. The book teaches how temporary setbacks inspire you to improve and get better, eventually bringing you out of "the dip."

Learning this at a young age shaped my mentality in a way that prepared me for the adversity that was to come. My mother used to say, "I have more faith in what's above your shoulders than what's below them." My siblings and I always sighed when she said this because we all wanted to play professional sports. After experiencing season-ending injuries, we immediately understood what she was saying.

Nevertheless, we did not allow our injuries to discourage us. The drive and mental willpower that were instilled in us allowed us to seek out opportunities that led us to where we are today. Whether I was an intern or a CEO, this mindset helped me figure out that if I am in a Dip that's worthy of my time, effort, and talents, the old saying is wrong—winners do quit, and quitters do win, but if you can't lose, then you can't win.

Just Me

When it comes to just me, a ton of components make up who I am—life experiences, beliefs, philosophies. My father, Rudy Sr., is the biggest inspiration in my life and the reason I am the man I am today. We have the same name, for crying out loud. My father worked at Grady Hospital, where he met my mother, for years in the radiology department. My mother was able to stay home for five years and just take care of me and my siblings, so I've always admired what he was able to do for our family.

During my freshman year in college, my father passed from a stroke, and during that time I felt that I needed more hands-on application rather than rely on the lectures I was receiving in class. I decided to start a social enterprise, which later became a nonprofit, with my friends in school, who are still my friends to this day. That one decision set me on a path—or I should say an adventure—which would change my life for the better. Three years after my father passed, I received another blessing that changed my life for the better: a son. Becoming a father is a tough thing to explain, but for me, my son is the best accountability partner I could have ever asked for.

My son's birth brought out the best in everyone the day he was born. My brothers and sister received their first nephew, and my mother received her first grandchild. At just the age of twenty-two, I began to see the importance of why God created us and the value of purpose. My entire life, I thought that college would be the deciding factor to inspire this, but everyone's journey is different. I remember hearing one of my professors once say that in life, you could be six feet from gold, so just keep digging.

You can imagine that a young twenty-two-year-old, fresh out of college, wants to travel, jump into their career, or just have fun; the last thing they want to do would probably be a parent. I was actually blessed to do all of those things and never looked at becoming a father as a roadblock. I started working at Delta Airlines three months before my son was born and vowed to only travel to serve my purpose. Planting purposeful seeds over those next few years allowed me and my son to bond like no other. He accompanied me at community projects, business meetings, and study sessions. I honestly felt that God sent him to heal my family. Today, my son is a young man of God, an outstanding scholar, a tremendous athlete, and just an all-around great kid.

Volunteerism Beginnings

Attending church was something my family did not play about. While my father was more of the "go to work on Sundays" type, my mother was the one to make sure her children were at church faithfully. Don't get me wrong—even though my dad didn't attend church, he was a very spiritual individual and kept God first at all times. They both made sure to instill in me and my siblings the spirit of servitude. I can remember my mother upholding roles in the church such as secretary, Sunday school teacher, and more. We watched her lead the choir and even facilitate summer camps for the church. I can remember my father purchasing vehicles from used car lots and giving them to neighbors, family members, and friends from the kindness of his heart. These were the first principles that were instilled in me as a boy and set me on the path of becoming a global servant.

Today, I have been blessed to travel the word and serve others the same way I witnessed my parents serve. My desire to make a positive impact is reliant on those who I serve. No specific project or initiative will end suffering or eliminate the sadness that plagues our world, but serving on a consistent basis makes all the difference. There are countless ideas on how to save the world, but a great number of them need assistance to do so. Working in the philanthropy space has provided me with a countless number of opportunities to serve the individuals I seek to serve. When the people you serve truly know that the results of your impact really work, the smiles on their faces become more valuable than gold. When clean water can be provided daily as compared to monthly, lives are able to continue. When resources are provided to first-generation college students, you can now equip the next generation with properly trained leadership. These acts of service are what drive me every day, and I work to normalize an atmosphere of love and progression for all those who seek it. Consistency is key.

July 2021 was my first mission trip. That month, I served in Haiti and Ghana, my first time in both countries. I grew up always wanting to visit Africa and had little knowledge of Haiti until I became older. The first trip that month was to Haiti, where my team and I served for a week, assisting local schools and orphanages with daily chores and providing health kits to the youth. The economic structure of the lands served absolutely blew my mind.

I had only witnessed poverty from the American perspective, but what I saw during my time in Haiti was far worse. Entire families living on sidewalks inside of structures built from whatever they could find. People hopping on the back of trucks just to make it up the road or to the next city. Men, women, and children selling goods to whoever was willing to patronize them. All of this took place with hundreds of people maneuvering through the streets on the way to their destinations.

I was blessed with the opportunity to give a young nineteen-year-old a haircut and talk about his viewpoints on his country's current state and what his goals were. He voiced that it was tough growing up and maintaining a social life with friends and family due to the country's current state. He said that he was grateful for the school he attended and had plans of moving to the states when he could. I commended him for his strength and encouraged him that everything was going to work out for good because he wanted it to. Those great conversations and experiences in Haiti paved the way for the next trip to Ghana.

My team and I spent a week in Accra and a week in Cape Coast, where we participated in the Pan African Festival. We had the opportunity to lead career workshops for local college students, attend traditional ceremonies, and even sail across the Atlantic from where our ancestors were sold in slavery. My appreciation for life excelled in this trip because I was able to see where my people came from and how they made it back. The people of Ghana referred to us as the stolen children. They greeted us as brothers and sisters, which honestly made me feel like I was returning back home.

One of the most memorable experiences I have from that trip is the tour of the slave dungeons. From the moment I stepped foot on the property, I felt my ancestors' memories of the horrific environment. I can recall our tour guide explaining in detail the process of how our people were tortured and how it made me feel during the tour. I remember him saying, "When you came in here, it was a death sentence." That one phrase has stuck with me to this day and has driven me in my service work.

The Ripple Effect

While my global service work made a great impact on those I served, the ripple effect on family members, friends, and colleagues was even more profound when I returned home. There were so many thoughts and plans I wanted to execute when I returned, but I was more excited about spending time with loved ones and identifying ways I could create heart-warming experiences for others. "Change cannot be forced; it can only be inspired" came from Simon Sinek's book *Start With Why* and has been a building block for my perspective. Channeling one's inspiration into others can be a challenge sometimes because everyone serves differently. Some serve through donations, while others serve hands-on. Some serve through social media engagement, and others may provide affirming compliments to the work being done. All of these methods are accepted in the world of philanthropy. The ripple effect from my global service work inspired me with seven principles that helped me inspire change to those around me.

The first inspirational principle was **patience**. In the early days of my entrepreneurial journey, I was very ambitious and felt that success was based on my performance; if I did not see quick results, then I was not applying myself. I learned that when approaching goals that are bigger than us, we must not base our success from an earthly lens. The future is unseen and cannot be rushed. This is especially true when serving others.

We must take each day at a time and rejoice over the results we intend for ourselves and those we serve, no matter how big or how small. Patience is the art of remaining calm and composed in the face of adversity, delays, or uncertainty. It involves cultivating a mindset that allows you to endure challenges with grace and resilience. Patience is not a passive waiting game but an active, intentional choice to stay focused on your goals despite obstacles.

This ripple effect taught me how to shift my perspective and view waiting not as a hindrance but as an opportunity for growth in humanitarian development. I was able to discover strengths that come from embracing the present moment and understanding that not all progress has to happen quickly. Having a patient mindset involves acknowledging that setbacks are a natural part of everyone's journey and that true success often requires time and perseverance.

The second principle was **empathy**. Growing up, my parents made sure my siblings and I established a healthy perspective for how we saw life and that we always respected others' perspectives as we got older. I made sure to hone in on this principle while overseas and practiced the art of active listening, which is a key component of empathy. I discovered techniques to fully engage with those I was serving and made it a point for them to know that their thoughts and feelings were not only heard but truly understood. This principle really rippled into my personal life when I returned home because I was able to see how empathy contributed to the health and longevity of my personal relationships.

I discovered how acknowledging and validating the emotions of those close to me can lead to increased fellowship, trust, and overall well-being. I was also able to see the impact of empathy in my career. I began to see how empathetic leadership inspires a positive organizational culture, enhances teamwork, and improves communication amongst my colleagues. This principle became a catalyst for innovation and collaboration.

The third principle to create the ripple effect is **responsibility**. Carrying out any form of philanthropy goes beyond good intentions, especially when serving in underserved communities and countries; it involves a commitment to ethical, sustainable, and culturally sensitive practices. Serving overseas taught me the importance of staying informed about cultural changes, global trends, and best practices to continually improve my approach of contributing positive and respectful engagement amongst those I am serving.

Every location has a unique demographic and cultural structure, so it is important to make it one's responsibility to become aware of how to properly communicate. Carrying out the principle of *responsibility* is becoming flexible and responsive to the evolving needs of the communities you are serving. I was pushed to learn how to navigate cultural nuances and unexpected challenges with grace and humility. I was also responsible for prioritizing collaboration with like-minded individuals, working alongside community members to identify needs, develop solutions, and build capacity for sustainable change. This is the cornerstone of impactful philanthropy work.

The fourth principle is **independence**. While in Ghana, I observed how the citizens in the rural areas built and ran the operation of the communities they lived in rather than rely on their government, which only provided certain resources. Independence in this context does not imply isolation but emphasizes empowering communities to become self-sufficient and resilient. This was something I worked to inspire in my friends and family once I returned home.

We all have the ability to change the trajectory of our lives, and all it takes is effort. Everyone involved must address challenges, seize opportunities on their own, and discover methods for identifying and fostering local talent and expertise. Every community consists of these attributes along with emerging leaders who can provide mentorship and opportunities that empower individuals to take on leadership roles and drive positive change.

The fifth principle is **leadership**. This particular ripple showed me the importance of visionary and servant leadership in mission work. My team and I were fueled with purpose from the vision that was initially established. That vision transcended any challenges we faced, providing a clear sense of direction for the mission trip. I was able to learn how to communicate a vision that resonated with both my team and the communities we served through this way of thinking.

Servant leadership embraces the needs of others, serving as catalysts for positive change. Through this form of leadership, my team and I learned how to cultivate a mindset of humility and genuine care for the well-being of everyone involved. Putting oneself after others creates an atmosphere of love and allows inspiration to freely flow. This would have to be one of my most favorite principles, mainly because it can be applied in every aspect of life.

The sixth principle is **mindfulness**. As much as I wanted to think of home while serving abroad, I had to remain in the moment and give my undivided attention to the work at hand. Mindfulness involves being fully present in the moment and approaching challenges with a focused and compassionate mindset. This mindset allowed for respectful interactions with the diverse communities and assisted my approach with curiosity toward the cultural differences I encountered.

I have always understood the importance of decision-making and its potential impact, considering both short-term and long-term consequences. The secret sauce to decision-making is being mindful of those consequences. The ripple effect of what I learned doing mission work has affected my life more than I could have ever imagined, and it all started with a moment.

The seventh and final principle is **balance**. For me, this is definitely a guiding principle that enhances all aspects of my life and elevates the effectiveness of my service work. By striking a balance in mission objectives and personal well-being, I have been able to successfully navigate the complexities of humanitarian work.

Prioritizing self-care to maintain physical, emotional, and mental health during long hours on your feet, while out in the element, or just even while facilitating organizational experiences is very important. I learned how to set boundaries for a healthy work-life balance that helped me sustain effectiveness in the field. If done correctly, the engagement you have in the community will not only be memorable but ever the more satisfying due to a healthy state of being.

As we close, I am filled with a great sense of gratitude for the journey we've shared. These pages have unfolded to reveal a life shaped by the threads of family, spirituality, and a career devoted to my philanthropic pursuits. Family is the cornerstone of my existence, the source of enduring love, support, and shared laughter. Through the highs and lows, I've learned to embody a spirit of resilience and the profound joy that comes from belonging. These chronicle the lessons learned, the bonds strengthened, and the growth that stems from the unconditional love of those who walk beside us on this journey. We have ventured into the depths of my spirituality and my connection with the things unseen and greater than ourselves.

Through moments of reflection and spiritual awakening, I have discovered the transformative power of faith. Lastly, the ripple effect of my career in the community unfolds as a purposeful step-by-step methodology to servicing humanity. From the first principles of establishing one's internal approach to the evolving strategies aimed at making a positive impact, this journey has been a testament to the resilience of the human spirit.

As I express gratitude for the chapters that have been written, I also recognize that this story is ongoing. The narrative continues to evolve, shaped by the experiences yet to come. I extend my deepest appreciation to all those who have been part of this journey—family, friends, colleagues, and the communities we've served together.

Looking forward, I carry the lessons, memories, and values etched into the pages of this anthology. May the stories shared within these covers inspire others to embark on their own quests for purpose and meaningful contributions to the world. As the final pages turn, I am filled with a sense of fulfillment and anticipation for what's to come. May your own stories be filled with a commitment to making the world a better place.

With Heartfelt Gratitude,

Rudy A. Simpson Jr.

Rudy A. Simpson Jr.

Chapter 10

Faith Without Ceasing

In the Beginning

I love serving the Lord because He has brought me a mighty long way! I'm the Pastor of the World Fellowship of Jesus Christ in McDonough, Georgia. I enjoy my faith because the Lord has been a blessing to me all my life, even when I did not even know it.

My journey started in a little town called Bluffton, Indiana. It's about twenty-four miles southwest of Fort Wayne, Indiana. This is where my faith journey began. I was just five years old. I was blessed to have the family that I have. My wonderful parents are Martha Rowe and Jimmy Ray Adkins. I'm the youngest of five children. My parents were from the southern states. Dad was from Mississippi, and my mother is from Kentucky. As you can probably imagine, we were raised in a traditional southern household. We were taught to be mannerable, to love each other, and to do our part to strengthen our family.

I am the baby of five children. Even though I was the youngest, I remember when my parents divorced. This was my first heartbreak. I remember feeling like a fish out of water when my parents separated. I remember experiencing challenging times with both of them separately. I love them both unequivocally. Soon after my parents divorced, my mother moved to Fort Wayne, Indiana.

My brother Jimmie, sisters Lucia and Mia, and I moved with my mother during the beginning of the divorce. My sister Evelyn lived in Jackson, Mississippi, with her mother. A few months later, my brother Jimmie and I moved back to Bluffton with our dad. My dad, brother, and I all lived with my grandparents, Effie and Tommy Green, in a one-bedroom apartment next to my grandmother. We lived on top of a True Value Hardware building in downtown Bluffton. I had some great times in Bluffton. The good Lord always would speak to me, but I didn't know Him like I know Him now. Jehovah would teach me things like fishing, coon hunting, and the ability not to hold any grudges or have any issues with people. I remember quite frankly being the only Black student in class because Wells County Community Schools were predominantly white, and at some point, we were one of two Black families in the entire city.

Once again, the Lord always looked out for me. While attending the schools in that community, the teachers always attempted to improve my speaking and academic abilities. I grew up with a lisp. The schools in that county helped me speak better by working on my sounds, which helped to make my lisp seem less noticeable. I still have a slight lisp to this day, but it's not as noticeable as it was when I was younger.

Something happened to me when I was approximately nine years old. I remember my father waking me up and saying, "Hey. We're going to Mississippi. I want you to meet your sister."

I said to my dad, "Are you referring to one of my sisters in Fort Wayne?"

He said, "No. I'm talking about your sister, Evelyn Robinson, in Jackson, Mississippi."

I will never forget when we appeared at her doorstep with her mom, Helen. My dad said, "Meet your sister, Evelyn," and we have been great siblings ever since. Once again, God has always looked out for me. Evelyn has been as important to me as my other sisters. I have wonderful sisters; the Lord has always used them to watch over me and keep me out of trouble. They also advised me on doing certain things, and they made sure I hit my books when I was in school.

Approximately two years later, my father met a young lady named Selena from Anderson, Indiana, and we relocated to Fort Wayne, Indiana, with her son, Dwayne. Selena was a good lady, but she and my dad did not stay together, and my father ended up raising my brother and me on Eckart Street in Fort Wayne to a certain extent. Now, this is how good God is: While in Fort Wayne, we were able to spend an extraordinary amount of time with my mother, who was a successful businessperson and did a lot of things in the community. She gave me a lot of insight to this day on how to be a business person. We were so blessed that we were raised by both of our parents . . . again. God was always looking out for me all through my middle school and high school years. I saw both of my parents every day even though they lived in two different homes. I experienced both the hood life and the suburban life.

My dad was pretty complacent with the lifestyle that he had, but my mother, bless her heart, was always striving to do better every day. I applaud her for that because God used her to show me the other side of the world. She has sent me to many different places and has done so much for me that I was able to see that there is light at the end of any tunnel. Now, my brothers and sisters are wonderful people, and they enjoy life to the extent of extreme happiness.

While growing up in Fort Wayne, Indiana, we had some great experiences. The city used to have great activities, such as the Black Expos, which were wonderful celebrations of family and culture; they brought people together. This was and still is a great place to be raised. There were many of those experiences during my early childhood years. I would always take a step back, and the Lord always looked out for me and would take me a step forward.

In middle school, I would work hard, and then go home and study. I had a pretty rough time because I was always getting bullied—not the kind of bullying we have today but bullying as far as playing the dozens. I wasn't good at it until I got to high school. If you're not familiar with playing the dozens, it's when you're in a verbal competition with jokes involving one or more people. It usually entails having a crowd of people as an audience laughing or *ooh*ing and *aah*ing.

Eventually, I became the main guy playing the dozens and still am to this day, but I do it for fun. While attending high school, I was inspired by a good friend of mine named Oliver Richmond and my best friends, Eddie Dixon and John Domonick Dixie. These gentlemen helped to shape me into the man I am today along with Tim Martin, JoJo Thomas, Sydney Sherrell, Richard Jordan, Nate Alexander, Robert Davis Jr., and a host of wonderful neighborhood friends who helped in raising me. I am grateful for the people who poured into my life.

"I Can Do All Things Through Christ the Lord, Who Strengthens Me." — *Philippians 4:13*

One of the things that the Lord has always done for me is give me the ability to want to do better with myself. I did that by playing sports. I wasn't that good at all, but it gave me a sense of camaraderie and the ability to have a sense of worth. My siblings were older than me, so they hung out with a different crowd.

Being the baby in the family, I would always spend time with my mom and dad. I would frequently go back to Bluffton, Indiana, to spend time with one of my best friends. He was a young man named Gerald Williams.

The Lord sent people in my life to guide me, protect me, and love me. I recognize that now. As a man of the cloth, there could have been many opportunities for me to make a decision that could have changed the course of my life, BUT GOD. God has shown me favor through and through. I honor the Lord with my talents, teachings, and time.

"The Lord is my shepherd; I shall not want. He maketh me to lie down in green pastures: he leadeth me beside the still waters. He restoreth my soul: he leadeth me in the paths of righteousness for his name's sake. Yea, though I walk through the valley of the shadow of death, I will fear no evil: for thou art with me; thy rod and thy staff they comfort me."
— Psalms 23:1–4

I would go visit my grandmother to eat Thanksgiving and Christmas meals and put up Christmas lights. There are certain seasons I really enjoy, and I miss my grandmother dearly because of those times we spent together. Visiting her ensured that I had a great holiday experience. During those times back in Fort Wayne, I played baseball and football, wrestled, and ran track. I wasn't that good, but God always looked out for me.

I had some good friends over the years whom I'm still close to. I had the pleasure of spending time with them while we were on the same teams. One of the greatest things that happened to me was that I became a high school wrestler. It's very competitive. Some of the best times of my life were when I won conference championships and was able to compete at a high level for my high school.

My good friend Oliver Richmond was a two-time state champion. He helped mold me into being the best wrestler I could have been. Although I did not win the state championship, one of the greatest awards I ever received was Best Mental Attitude. My coach, Jim Wellborn, was an excellent coach whose quality in coaching and training made athletes become the best that they could be. This helped me to continually strive to be the very best that I could be in life. As a result, I became very competitive in getting good grades. I was always competing against my best friend, Ed Dixon; he and I met in the fourth grade, and we always were competitive and held each other up.

We often talk about how good the Lord is and how He put in us the ability to discern what we should and shouldn't do. We both believe this kept us away from a lot of the issues that some of our colleagues had while we were growing up. When I was a young man, I lost a lot of friends to death and prison. God always looked out for me and my buddies, making sure we were moving on so we could be an inspiration to the world.

One of the tragedies that happened in my life when I was younger was when my siblings and I were skating at Roller Dome North in Fort Wayne, Indiana; I believe it's located on Coliseum Boulevard. We were rushed out of the skating rink to be notified that my mother had been shot by her estranged boyfriend, who had been extremely jealous of her. My heart broke because my mother was at the top of her game in her businesses, and she did a great job of trying to take care of us while working. At the same time, it was a very intense situation for a mother who was divorced and doing her best to make a good life for herself and her kids.

Raising four children and having this kind of setback must have been daunting for her, but I was so proud of my mother because after she was shot, she drove herself to the hospital. Thankfully, the bullets were not fatal, and my mother is still alive, healthy, and vibrant to this day. God has always looked out for me.

"For all that is in the world—the desires of the flesh and the desires of the eyes and pride of life—is not from the Father but is from the world."
— 1 John 2:16.

When I graduated from Elmhurst High School in Fort Wayne, Indiana, I graduated as an honor student with a full-ride scholarship to attend Indiana University. This was provided to me by Lincoln National Life Insurance Company. While in college, I did a few internships with the business, and I'm so grateful to them for investing in me to be the best that I can be as a student. I thought I didn't need God because things were going well for me, but my life was restored with my parents, and going to college was something I dreamed of doing. I was not sure if it was something that I could attain. I had real good friends who made it out of the hood and were able to experience the suburban life yet were empty inside.

I wasn't proud of some of the things that I did. I never was a heavy drinker, but I began to dabble a little bit. Once in college, my troubles began. I had an interest in the party life and the ladies. I didn't go to school and do what I was supposed to do. Instead of spending the majority of my time studying, I was enjoying my time partying. I pledged Kappa Alpha Psi Fraternity, and boy, did we party! I was involved in many activities on campus, and I enjoyed being around people.

I was a social magnet, but I jumped into relationships with ladies whom I barely knew and began to have children with them. I took care of one child for two years who, as I found out later, was not my child. Then, I had my son, Brenndon, while I was a senior at Indiana University. I didn't learn my lesson the first time; I was still very promiscuous and enjoyed being around the ladies. A lot of this led to my demise. Instead of being focused on the right things, I was focused on the wrong things.

While in college and having children, I worked three jobs, joined the Indiana University Army ROTC, and became a U.S. Army officer. The motivation behind this was to help take care of my children while I was in school. It did not work out; my first son's mother and I broke up shortly after our son was born, and I began a life of struggles.

In 1991, after I graduated from college in December 1990, I was on my way to an officer basic course at Fort McClellan in Alabama, not having any idea that I could get deployed for the war. I was really confused because I had one son, and I just was not focused, but God always looked out for me. The war was short-lived, and I finished my officer basic course and went back to Indiana University to finish out the lease for the apartment I shared with my colleagues.

"In the world, you will have tribulation.
But take heart; I have overcome the world." — John 16:33

While there, I met my wonderful wife, LaChelle, but we didn't hit it off at first. We were close, but I never told her how much I cared about her, and things didn't work out in the beginning. Well, in July of 1991, I was saved by the Lord Jesus Christ. I gave my life to Him even though I had ups and downs in my past. During this time, I contacted Lachelle, who was not my wife at the time. I told her that I was saved. She told me that she always wanted to marry a man who was saved. We started dating again. We tried to keep our hands off each other, but we couldn't.

I moved to Louisville, Kentucky, with my mother because she had to relocate there to help sell our family's hair care products. While there, I was struggling financially, so I decided to go look for a job back in Fort Wayne. God always looked out for me. I was going to take a job I will never forget for $28,500. It was not enough to pay back my student loans. That amount was a little more than enough to take care of my son, Brenndon, and so I started backsliding. I moved back in with my sister in Fort Wayne for a very short time, and within one month, once again, I found out that Lachelle was pregnant. We weren't married at the time. I will never forget. I was sitting on my sister's steps when she gave me a phone call and told me that she was pregnant. I told her that I would be responsible. I love her so much.

I went back to Indiana University and started graduate work in the School of Education, and we had plans to get married at the time. There were some disagreements about our marriage, so I moved out of our apartment and moved in with some colleagues.

Once again, it was like circles, right? I kept doing the same thing over and over again, but God always took care of me.

In July of 1992, my daughter, Taylor, was born. It changed me; I had a girl now. I was looking at all the things that I'm not proud of that I had done with ladies and realized that I had a *daughter*. I wanted to prevent her from experiencing guys like me. I ran through some very difficult times once again. I moved out and started hanging out with my buddies again, partying again. The backsliding over and over again is the same old story.

This particular time, I was in the wrong place at the wrong time, and I had found that this was not the life I wanted to live. So, I went over to Lachelle's apartment, got on bended knee, and asked her to marry me again—and she said yes!

I moved back in with her, and in January of 1993, we got married. We've been married for thirty-one years now, and the story doesn't stop there. Approximately two weeks after I proposed to Lachelle, I got a call from a young lady named Deshawn Hale. She told me that she was late. I did not know what she was referring to.

I said, "Do you need a ride?"

She said, "No. I'm *late*. I'm pregnant."

My life took a turn, I believe, for the worst—or was it for the better? Now, I had found the love of my life, I had a child who was not my wife's child, and I had another child who was going to be born in the middle of my first year of marriage. This was the first time in my life that I wanted to get on an airplane, go to Jamaica, and never come back to America.

I was not the kind of guy that would quit, so I stuck it out. My son with Deshawn was born with Cerebral Palsy. His name is Christian. She is a hero, and she has spent the majority of her life raising our son. I am so grateful for her. She is a wonderful person. She's educated, and she is a magnificent example of a mother to a child with special needs.

"But they that wait upon the LORD shall renew their strength; they shall mount up with wings as eagles; they shall run, and not be weary; and they shall walk, and not faint." — Isaiah 40:29–31

Over the years, I ended up having twelve more children by my wife, making me a father to a total of thirteen children by my wife and two other children by two other ladies, giving me fifteen children. My children by my wife are Taylor, Jonathan, Alexandria, Mackenzie, Victoria, Elisabeth, Olivia, Danielle, Jeremiah, Joshua, Jordan, Faith, and Hope.

I am so grateful for all of my children despite the challenges and circumstances that were raised against me. God has always been good to me. I've had many trials and tribulations, from cars repossessed and homes foreclosed to losing money in business. I am educated, I've had wonderful jobs, and I work for three of the top five companies in America. I retired as a Major in the United States Army.

I've raised my children in my home, ten of whom live with me now. Several of them are educated, and some have their own businesses. I am a pastor at church. I'm telling you I know God is awesome! Why? Because He will take care of those who seek him.

He rewards them diligently, and He never gives up on his children. He always looks out for us.

I love the Lord because He first loved me. I can't put everything in this chapter, but I can tell you I can write 30,000 books about how good God has been to me. I've had tough times, I've had good times, and I'm glad God has never given up on me. He has always been there for me, and He has always allowed me to be the best I can be.

Most people talk to me and look at me but never think that I've had the life that I have had. I've been very successful, my kids are successful, my wife is successful, and my church is successful. God has replaced the shaky foundation that I once had with a solid foundation, and that's his son Jesus Christ. He's always looked out for me . . . always! He's allowed me to reconcile. I don't have grudges. I just love the fact that God makes me a peaceful guy who tries my very best to be the best version of myself.

My challenge is for anyone who reads this chapter to realize that no matter what you go through in life, if you put your trust in God, you don't have to worry about anything, and I mean that. I'm not just telling you some fairytale story. God has blessed me with houses and cars, given me ideas, and given me money. He's given me thousands of dollars from what seems to be out of nowhere. He keeps me in good health and allows me to pursue happiness. He's delivered me out of depression. He's taken me out of sorrow and delivered me when I didn't even think I could be delivered. He's given me the courage to get out and speak the truth about what He has done for me. I just want to continue to be a big enough light even though I still have shortcomings. I have a lot of work to do. God is there for me, and I love Him for that.

May God bless you, and I pray that this chapter has been an inspiration for you.

Pastor Jerome Adkins

The Phenomenal Book Series

Phenomenal Stories Lived by Phenomenal Men & Women

The *Phenomenal* book series was created as a platform for individuals to share their stories of God's glory. Throughout the twelve-week process, authors receive a one-hour virtual book coaching session that covers story development, best writing practices, legal terms, feedback on chapter content, community writing sessions, and book marketing. We also bring in guest speakers!

This writing experience is ideal for first-time authors who want to learn about the writing and publishing industry. Many of the participants are enthused to have a community of like-minded co-authors that are in the cohort, the sense of community aids in accomplishing their writing goals! Once each book is published, authors have the option to expand their chapters into an entire book since there are no restrictions outlined in the publishing contract. To learn more about this series, visit www.bffpublishinghouse.com

The Phenomenal Book Series:

Phenomenal Faith: Here Because I Was Healed
Phenomenal Favor: Here Because I Was Chosen
Phenomenal Men of Faith

The BFF Publishing House Team

Antionette "Toni" Mutcherson, MBA remembers falling in love with writing and literature as a young child. She credits her mother and schoolteachers for planting the seeds of reading and writing within her as an elementary-age student. Toni presented a TEDx Talk, "One Mom's Quest to Win Back Her Child from YouTube," in November 2019, on the importance of childhood literacy.

In 2013, Toni published the first of three children's books in the *Adventures of Jett Antoinette* book series, inspired by her nine-year-old daughter, Jett. The highlight of Toni's career is when she and her team published over 200 Black American children ages 6 to 17 from all across the country for free in the anthologies, *My Young Life Matters: The Next Generation Speaks* in 2020 and *My Young Life Matters II: Poetic Injustice* in 2022. The young authors received writing resources that helped them to become award-winning, best-selling authors.

In 2007, Toni graduated from Clark Atlanta University with a bachelor's degree in Business Administration, and in 2017, she received her master's degree in Business Administration from Florida Agricultural and Mechanical University. Toni is an active member of Delta Sigma Theta Sorority, Incorporated. She lives in Atlanta, Georgia.

In 2022, Toni founded the Crystal Stair Group 501C3, a nonprofit organization dedicated to the advancement and promotion of Black excellence in an array of industries, including literacy, social justice, technology, community development, entrepreneurship, and the arts.

As an advocate for children's literacy, she lives by the mantra, "Readers are leaders." To find out more about Antionette "Toni" Mutcherson, visit www.bffpublishinghouse.com.

Riel Felice graduated from Florida State University in 2020 with a Bachelor of Science degree in Media/Communications Studies and a Bachelor of Arts degree in Editing, Writing, and Media. In addition, Riel was a Spring 2019 initiate into the Kappa Epsilon Chapter of Delta Sigma Theta Sorority, Incorporated.

Riel is a professional editor with heavy experience; in her work with five publishing houses, she has edited numerous books of varying genres, in addition to screenplays, blog posts, magazine articles, social media content, and more. She possesses an unmatched adoration for the written word.

Riel loves to center herself in her spirituality through activities such as yoga and meditation; spend quality time with loved ones; indulge in self-care; enjoy picnics on the beach; and, ultimately, explore and experience the world through eyes that perceive the unconditional love in all things and all people. For more information and to connect with Riel, visit www.rielfelice.com.